The Ultimate Activity Book for
SMART GIRLS

Tricky Brain Teasers, Mind Games and Logic Puzzle Activities for Girls 8-12

IQ Street

Copyright © 2024 By Curious Press

979-8-89095-043-7

ALL RIGHTS RESERVED

No part of this book may be reproduced, stored in a retrieval system, or transmitted in any form or by any means, including electronic, mechanical, photocopying, recording, scanning, or otherwise without the prior written permission of the publisher.

The illustrations in this book were designed using images from Freepik.com.

Table of Contents

Introduction 01
Activities 02
Conclusion 112
Solutions 113

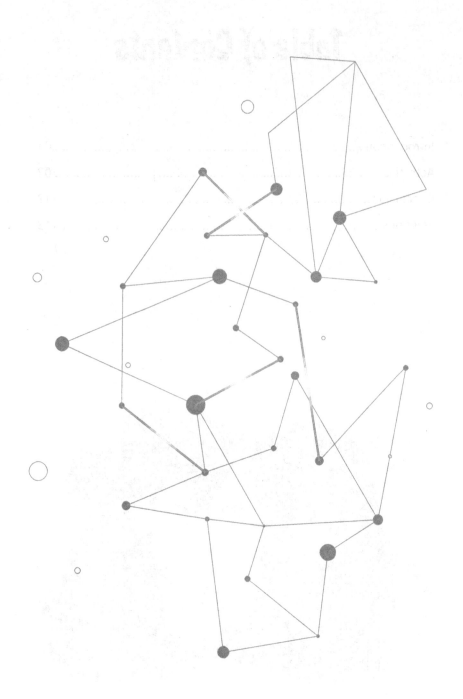

Introduction

Who doesn't like solving puzzles?

Whether it's unscrambling a word jumble, solving a crossword clue, hunting down words in a word search, or figuring out some mind-bending connection in a logic game, puzzles and brain teasers not only give your gray matter a little mental workout—they're a lot of fun too!

But how often do you sit down to solve a puzzle or a word game and find them... well, a little on the easy side? How often do you find yourself wanting a slightly trickier challenge or a slightly tougher mental workout? If that sounds familiar, then this book is just for you!

Welcome to *The Ultimate Activity Book for Smart Girls*. Inside here, you'll find over 100 pages of fun and challenging word games, picture puzzles, number challenges, matching games, and lots, lots more—all specially designed with you, a super smart girl, in mind!

To ease you in, the first few games here will introduce some of the different kinds of puzzles and games that you're going to encounter in the rest of this book. These first few puzzles won't be as big or as difficult as some of the others—this is really just a little introductory chance for you to learn the rules, pick up some tips, and warm up that puzzle-solving brain of yours!

After that, though, page by page we'll slowly make things a little tougher, until the final few games and activities here will push your puzzle-solving brain to its limits! (Flick ahead to puzzle number 100 to see what you have in store!)

Don't worry if you get stuck at any point along the way, though. At the back of the book, you'll find all the solutions to the puzzles and games—so if you just want to double-check an answer you're unsure of or want a helping hand to make a start, all the answers are right there.

So let's get going! Grab a pen or a pencil, and let's tackle your first fiendish challenge...

-1-

One of the different kinds of puzzles you'll come across in this book is a classic word search. Some of the puzzles here will have a little twist, making them a little harder than they might first appear ... but let's start things off more straightforwardly with this puzzle all about the mall. Can you find these 15 words and phrases in the grid of letters below? The answers might be hidden upwards or downwards, backwards and forwards, and diagonally in any direction—but always in a straight line.

L	U	O	V	N	V	Z	F	S	D	B	F	L	Y	I	K	F
U	U	P	X	V	Z	A	R	O	O	P	Q	L	I	C	F	P
L	C	J	L	J	N	O	X	O	U	E	T	L	J	F	A	L
F	A	U	J	A	T	S	K	O	F	N	Z	N	X	R	S	A
U	D	G	P	A	Z	S	C	W	W	T	T	W	D	C	H	S
W	L	J	V	K	T	A	U	C	G	A	F	A	V	K	I	T
Z	T	E	T	O	M	S	E	H	T	O	L	C	I	U	O	I
N	L	D	R	A	S	A	L	O	N	B	W	K	N	N	N	C
E	O	E	Z	Q	G	R	G	G	E	P	H	Z	I	L	M	P
K	S	E	I	R	E	C	O	R	G	U	M	W	V	N	W	L
U	O	C	Y	N	E	O	G	T	X	J	Q	P	F	U	G	A
Q	Y	T	T	U	R	A	L	U	A	D	Y	I	V	E	Z	N
M	H	H	E	B	Y	W	A	S	T	L	G	Z	T	F	S	T
N	Q	U	E	D	F	V	S	A	O	N	A	F	C	U	G	S
P	P	G	A	L	P	H	S	X	O	A	A	C	W	E	O	T
C	D	A	O	F	O	O	D	C	O	U	R	T	S	F	Z	B
C	O	P	T	O	L	G	N	I	K	R	A	P	N	E	D	F

BOOKSTORES | BOUTIQUE | CLOTHES | ELEVATORS | ESCALATORS | FASHION | FOOD COURTS | FOUNTAIN | GLASS | GROCERIES | PARKING LOT | PLASTIC PLANTS | PLAZA | SALON | WALKING

− 2 −

This is a classic sudoku puzzle. To solve a sudoku, you need to fill out the numbered grid below so that each left-to-right row of nine squares, each top-to-bottom column of nine squares, and each smaller 3 x 3 set of nine squares (marked out in the heavy black lines) contains the digits 1–9 once and only once.

So there cannot be any duplicate numbers in a row, a column, or a set of the smaller squares. Given the numbers already in the grid, can you complete it correctly?

To start you off, take a look at the shaded row in the grid below. It is missing an 8—but because there's already an 8 in the middle 3x3 box on the bottom row (in bold), the 8 on the shaded row must go in the circled space on the left, because there can't be any duplicates! So go ahead and place an 8 in the circled box. After that, though, you're on your own...

		4		9		6	5	1
	9	6	5	8				7
		5	6					
6	5			7		9	1	
9	8	2	1		6			3
					3			6
5	4	◯	3			7	6	2
3		7			5		9	8
				7		8		5

- 3 -

Another type of puzzle in this book is a maze. Can you find your way through this fiendish full-page maze from one side to the other?

- 4 -

This next puzzle might look like normal a word search, but it has a peculiar twist!

The names of 10 hairstyles and hair-related words are hidden in this grid—but they're not in straight lines! Their letters can connect horizontally or vertically, and in any direction, backwards or forwards, upwards or downwards, but never diagonally.

Can you find all 10 answers, so that no letters are used more than once and there are no unused letters left over? The first answer has been filled in for you to make a start.

P	O	N	B	A	N	G	B
S	A	Y	I	H	C	S	U
Y	M	T	G	N	S	E	N
E	M	A	N	O	B	H	C
T	C	I	L	E	R	P	E
R	I	O	I	X	A	M	R
U	P	N	S	T	I	B	O
O	D	S	N	E	D	S	B

– 5 –

Here's an especially tricky challenge for you... This is a logic puzzle! Using the clues and the grid below, can you figure out the answer to this problem?

Four friends—Clara, Diedre, Ellie, and Frances—are looking around the clothes store. One of them is looking for a new jacket; another wants a new bag; someone wants a new T-shirt; and the fourth wants some new shoes. Each friend is looking at a different colored item too: one is black, another blue, one red, and a fourth white.

Based on the clues below, can you work out who is looking at what? The first clue has been filled in the grid already to show you how to solve this puzzle—and be sure to use the checklist grid at the bottom of the page as you go!

1. ~~Ellie is browsing for a new pair of shoes.~~
2. The friend who is looking for a new bag has a five-letter name...
3. ...while the person looking at the black jacket has a C in their name!
4. The T-shirt is red, but the bag is not white.

	Jacket	Bag	T-shirt	Shoes	Black	Blue	Red	White
Clara				✘				
Diedre				✘				
Ellie	✘	✘	✘	✓				
Frances				✘				
Black								
Blue								
Red								
White								

FRIEND	CLOTHING ITEM	COLOR
Clara		
Diedre		
Ellie	Shoes	
Frances		

– 6 –

This is a general knowledge acrostic puzzle! To solve it, you need to answer the 10 trivia questions listed here, then place their answers in the corresponding rows in the grid.

In this puzzle, all the answers have six letters. In the other acrostic puzzles in this book, the answers might be longer or shorter. But once the grid is complete, the first letter of each answer, in turn, will spell something out, reading down the shaded column—and in this puzzle, the solution is _____. What is it?

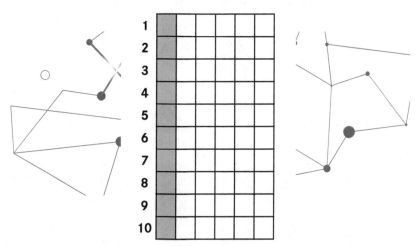

1. What device has a lens, a shutter and an aperture and might be fitted to a tripod?
2. In what US state would you find Honolulu?
3. What are there twelve of in a foot, and 36 in a yard?
4. What was the name of the terrifying gorgon in Greek mythology who had snakes for hair and could turn people who looked at her to stone?
5. What central American country is famous for its canal?
6. What was the first name of Queen Victoria's husband?
7. Hoover Dam is located on the border between Arizona and which other state?
8. By what name are the black-and-white striped horse-like animals of Africa known?
9. What is forty multiplied by two?
10. What word when used of a person means to die, but when used of food means to go out of date?

-7-

There are some classic quick crosswords in this book too. Use the corresponding ACROSS and DOWN clues on the next page to fill in the grid, with connecting words sharing the same the same letter. How quickly can you solve this puzzle?

ACROSS

1. Entrance to a room
5. Sets of two, like shoes or socks
8. Remarkable, exceptional
9. Person who has a pet
10. Hurt, was sharply painful
11. Asked for in a restaurant
12. Tugged
14. Sails effortlessly through the air
17. Sagged
19. Smelling organs
22. Remain in bed (two words)
23. First letter
24. Cheekily rude
25. Due to be married

DOWN

1. Amounts of medicine
2. Grand musical work for singers and an orchestra
3. Writhe
4. Lemon color
5. Happy with your accomplishments
6. Paid no attention to
7. Long steps or paces
12. Pools of rain water
13. Female big cat
15. Touching down
16. Help, instruction
18. One-cent piece
20. Rock back and forth
21. Dish of raw vegetables

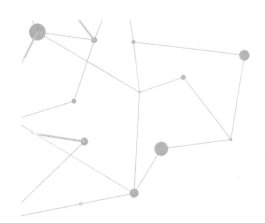

- 8 -

Another type of puzzle you'll come across in this book is this crisscross puzzle. Here, you'll be given a set of words, all which connect together in the grid. Unlike in a crossword, though, you won't be given clues to work out where the answers go—you'll have to work out where each one goes based only on how long it is and where it connects with the others! We're heading down to the coffee shop for this puzzle. Can you work out where all these words go?

BEANS	ESPRESSO	LATTE
CAPPUCCINO	EXTRA SHOT	MUFFIN
CHOCOLATE	HANDLE	MUG
DECAF	HOLDER	SERVICE
DRIP	ICED	TAKE OUT

– 9 –

Two 6-letter words—both the names of US states—have been jumbled together below. Can you work out what they are?

_ A _ _ _ _   _ _ _ A _ _

AAAADEKNNSSV

– 10 –

What four-word phrase has been coded into the picture below?

Answer _____

– 11 –

We're taking a trip to the beauty salon for this next word search puzzle. Can you find these 15 beauty treatments and salon terms in the grid below?

Y	V	R	V	J	G	Q	N	I	E	I	J	J	J	W	A	M
T	X	L	E	R	A	M	W	F	L	E	Y	V	J	H	W	A
W	I	N	C	V	T	B	W	S	R	I	A	M	F	H	E	S
G	N	Q	F	T	O	K	O	U	L	A	P	W	N	Y	J	S
P	A	I	K	Y	F	E	C	T	L	T	C	S	A	C	Y	A
O	E	A	B	O	G	I	K	I	O	O	X	I	T	R	U	G
E	B	Y	K	L	D	H	I	A	S	X	L	A	Y	I	R	E
S	R	C	D	E	O	P	R	M	M	Y	D	L	A	P	C	T
K	Y	U	P	R	S	W	E	H	H	P	U	A	R	I	Z	K
I	Q	G	C	T	I	T	D	J	A	T	A	J	P	X	G	S
N	L	Z	I	I	I	A	R	R	H	I	T	H	S	D	Y	X
C	F	C	I	C	N	D	H	I	Y	V	R	G	H	O	A	J
A	K	T	S	N	O	A	Q	W	C	P	I	S	J	O	K	B
R	X	E	A	W	L	M	M	P	H	Q	F	Z	T	E	D	N
E	N	I	I	A	M	H	P	H	Z	B	X	T	S	Y	I	U
A	L	W	F	Y	T	R	E	A	T	M	E	N	T	S	L	T
S	D	N	S	T	E	E	S	A	V	M	A	K	E	U	P	E

BLOW DRY | BOTOX | COSMETICS | HAIR DYE | HAIRSTYLE | LIPSTICK | MAKEOVER | MAKEUP | MANICURE | MASSAGE | NAILS | PEDICURE | SKINCARE | SPRAY TAN | TREATMENTS

– 12 –

Time for another sudoku. Fill in the grid below so that each row of nine squares, each column of nine squares, and each smaller 3 x 3 set of nine squares contain the digits 1–9 once and only once.

There can be no duplicate digits in any row, column, or smaller square.

Can you complete the grid correctly?

4	2	3			9		7	
8	1		2	3	6	9	5	4
			8			3	1	2
2		8	4		7	1		
			6	2	1		8	
1	5	4	9	8		2	6	
	4	5					9	
		2	3		8	5	4	1
			5	4	9	7		

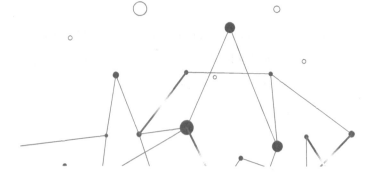

– 13 –

Can you find your way through this maze from one side to the other?

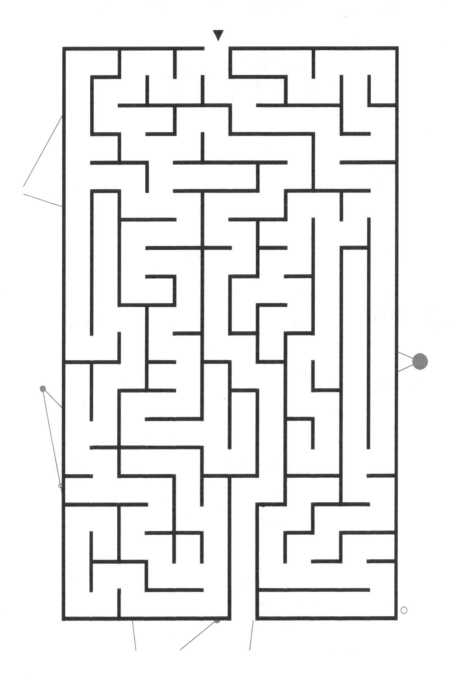

- 14 -

Using only the letters below, can you come up with one 7-letter word, two 6-letter words, three 5-letter words, and four 4-letter words?

U E Y S A D T

7 Letters _ _ _ _ _ _ _

6 Letters _ _ _ _ _ _   _ _ _ _ _ _

5 Letters _ _ _ _ _   _ _ _ _ _   _ _ _ _ _

4 Letters _ _ _ _   _ _ _ _

_ _ _ _   _ _ _ _

– 15 –

Every letter of the alphabet appears in the grid below at least twice—except two. One letter doesn't appear at all, and one letter appears only once, and so does not have a pair. Which are the odd ones out?

A	C	G	Z	B	L	D
S	I	Q	T	R	H	D
J	W	E	M	C	M	P
P	Y	F	T	W	K	V
N	U	Y	A	S	N	J
R	G	Z	X	I	E	X
B	L	V	F	H	Q	U

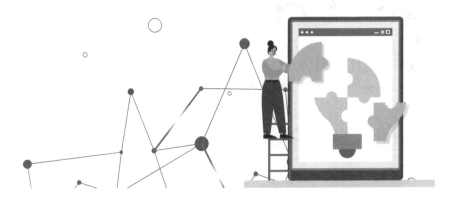

– 16 –

Listed on the left here are the names of eight Hollywood actresses. On the right are the names of eight films and film series in which they have starred. Can you match them together? The first answer has been filled in for you to make a start.

Gal Gadot — Wonder Woman

Kristen Wiig   The Lord of the Rings

Cate Blanchett   Bridesmaids

Emily Blunt   The Devil Wears Prada

Anne Hathaway   La La Land

Emma Stone   The Hunger Games

Saoirse Ronan   A Quiet Place

Jennifer Lawrence   Lady Bird

– 17 –

In this mini crossword, all the answers in the grid are anagrams of the clue words below. Can you unjumble them?

ACROSS 1. ROBED | **4.** SUES | **7.** CIVET | **8.** JETS | **9.** TRAMS | **11.** TOWER **15.** LOCO | **16.** TREED | **17.** SKAT | **18.** HEART.

DOWN 1. BARED | **2.** IRAN | **3.** TESTED | **5.** RESET | **6.** ITS | **10.** MELDED | **12.** TRIOS | **13.** CHARM | **14.** RATS | **15.** ACT.

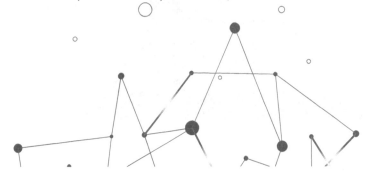

– 18 –

What four-word phrase has been coded into the picture below?

Answer _____

- 19 -

The theme of this crisscross puzzle is a birthday party. All 15 of these birthday-related words connect together in the grid below. Can you work out where they go?

BALLOONS
CAKE
CANDLES
CANDY
CARDS
DAY OUT
DECORATIONS
DRINKS
FAMILY
FRIENDS
FUN
GAMES
MUSIC
PARTY
PLAY
PRESENTS
SINGING
SURPRISE

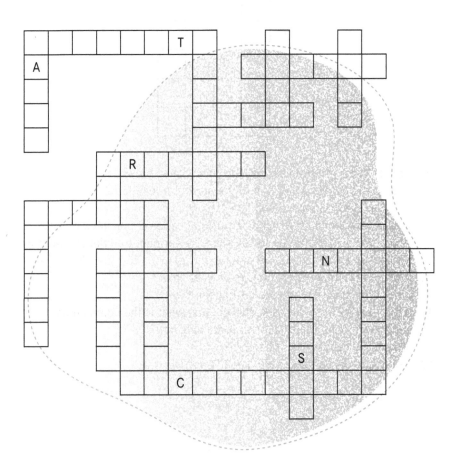

– 20 –

Place the 4-letter answers to the trivia questions below into the corresponding rows in the grid. Once complete, the name of a fruit will be spelled out down the shaded column.

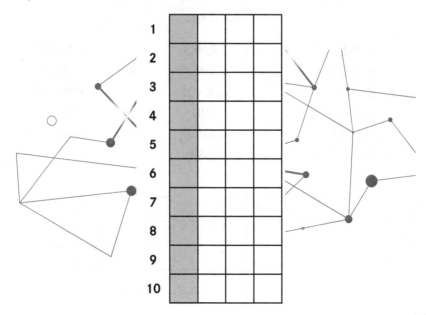

1. What kind of creature has species called black, brown, sun, and polar?
2. What is the female equivalent of the ancient title of lord?
3. Who was the first man in the Bible?
4. Lightning McQueen is a character in what series of animated movies?
5. What name is given to the tartan skirt-like garment traditionally worn in Scotland?
6. Cyan and ultramarine are shades of what color?
7. On a compass, what direction is opposite west?
8. Often seen on steel items kept outdoors, what is the common name of the oxidization of metallic items containing iron?
9. What is the capital city of Italy?
10. Complete this sentence: ME is to MY as YOU is to ... ?

– 21 –

Can you find your way through this maze from one side to the other?

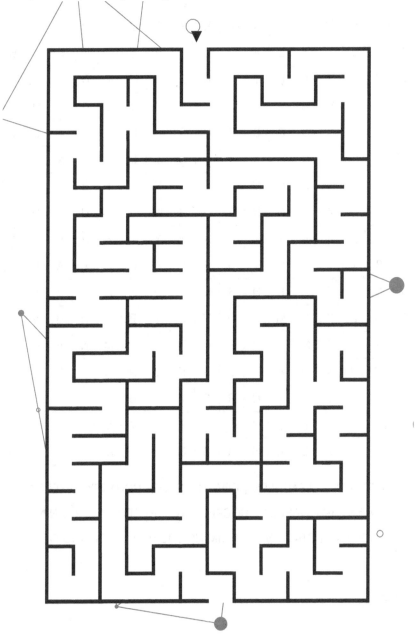

– 22 –

It's gym day at school! Can you find all these sports-related words and phrases in the grid?

C	Y	Y	W	F	F	A	M	K	Y	S	U	Q	M	S	X	L
G	H	N	J	T	E	A	M	Z	L	E	B	Y	T	R	L	W
U	N	K	X	X	K	T	H	R	E	V	H	R	D	A	V	G
G	N	I	M	M	I	W	S	S	I	Z	O	L	B	V	Q	Y
S	Z	E	N	D	D	B	X	G	F	P	E	T	S	A	G	R
T	V	F	J	N	H	X	Y	L	S	I	E	H	I	N	F	T
A	R	K	X	P	U	M	X	T	F	K	O	I	B	B	U	N
D	H	L	Z	K	N	R	E	D	S	W	U	X	U	L	N	U
I	D	Z	P	A	I	K	N	A	E	Y	E	F	M	E	Y	O
U	B	Y	S	Y	C	A	B	R	K	F	G	Z	L	A	B	C
M	X	I	T	A	K	H	S	S	M	N	Z	X	W	C	M	S
L	U	E	R	C	M	R	O	V	S	J	P	D	H	H	V	S
M	W	L	A	M	T	Q	R	C	N	E	C	M	N	E	O	O
D	M	R	W	U	W	I	S	S	K	G	N	O	G	R	O	R
E	T	Y	E	S	I	C	R	E	X	E	U	T	A	S	B	C
T	Y	V	W	P	J	Y	B	C	P	B	Y	V	I	C	N	P
F	A	X	X	L	K	H	X	S	S	L	D	M	F	F	H	A

BASKETBALL | BLEACHERS | COACH | CROSS COUNTRY | EXERCISE | FITNESS | GYMNASIUM | HOCKEY | RACKET SPORTS | RUNNING | SHOWERS | STADIUM | SWIMMING | TEAM | TRACK AND FIELD

- 23 -

Fill in the grid below so that each row of nine squares, each column of nine squares, and each smaller 3 x 3 set of nine squares contain the digits 1-9 once and only once.

There can be no duplicate digits in any row, column, or smaller square.

Can you complete the grid correctly?

9		1			5	7		3
				4		6		5
6	5	3	1	2	7			
5				6		9	4	2
1	9	4	2			3	7	
2	7			9	3			
			5	1	6	4		
	1		9	7				8
4	6			3	2	1		

– 24 –

The names of 14 European capital cities are hidden in this grid—but they're not in straight lines! They can connect horizontally or vertically, and in any direction, backwards or forwards, upwards or downwards, but never diagonally.

Can you find all the answers so that no letters are used more than once and there are no unused letters left over? The first answer has been filled in for you to make a start.

V	I	E	L	O	P	A	R	I	A
C	O	N	D	N	S	T	O	S	T
E	P	N	O	N	H	K	C	S	H
N	H	A	M	A	O	L	M	N	E
G	A	L	I	D	R	I	D	B	R
E	R	O	S	S	L	E	S	S	U
N	E	M	B	B	E	R	H	E	L
A	M	S	O	N	I	L	M	O	S
R	E	T	N	N	S	O	C	S	I
D	A	M	M	I	K	W	I	K	N

– 25 –

Here's another logic puzzle to wrap your head around.

It's a lazy Sunday morning, and four sisters—Jo, Kate, Lena, and Michelle—are each sitting about the house reading. One is reading a romance; another is reading a celebrity biography; a third is reading a classic novel; and a fourth is reading an adventure. One of the sisters is sitting in her bedroom; another in the garden; a third in the lounge; and a fourth is reading while she makes a cup of tea in the kitchen. Based on the clues below, can you figure out who is reading what and whereabouts around the house?

1. The sister who is reading in the kitchen has a 4-letter name.

2. Jo hates celebrity biographies!

3. The sister sitting in the lounge is reading the romance novel...

4. ...but that's not Jo, because she's still in bed!

5. Lena is reading her adventure story in the garden.

	Romance	Biography	Classic	Adventure	Bedroom	Garden	Lounge	Kitchen
Jo								
Kate								
Lena								
Michelle								
Bedroom								
Garden								
Lounge								
Kitchen								

SISTER	BOOK	ROOM
Jo		
Kate		
Lena		
Michelle		

– 26 –

How quickly can you solve this crossword?

ACROSS

1. Pile up, as on shelves
4. Black wood used to make piano keys
10. Road congestion
11. Solitary person
12. Admire
13. In the near past
15. America's longest river
19. Troops
20. Solid
23. Stadium
24. Everlasting
25. Posed a question
26. Passenger liner

DOWN

2. Athletics course, paired with field
3. Coffee shop
5. News update
6. Continuous
7. Not moving
8. Fashion items that accompany an outfit or complete a look
9. Medical images of bones
14. Guess
16. Disease
17. Customer's regular order
18. Little, petite
21. Internal
22. In this place

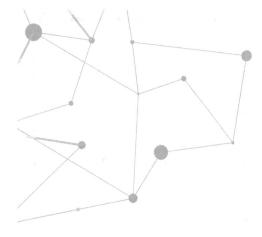

– 27 –

This is a spiral crossword. Each answer here begins in the corresponding numbered square—but the last letter of one answer is the first letter of the next, so that the entire crossword links together like a snake!

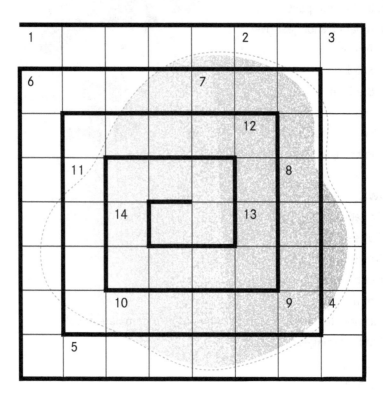

1. Multiply twofold
2. Day before a special event
3. Special ___, movie CGI
4. To the left or right
5. First day of the weekend
6. Belonging to you
7. Lucky number
8. Pleasant
9. Additional
10. Musician's collection of songs
11. Ground up, like meat
12. Performed, completed
13. Medic
14. Critic's opinion

– 28 –

Two 7-letter words—both the names of two-digit numbers—have been jumbled together here. What are they?

_ _ _ _ _ _ N   _ _ _ _ _ _ N

EEEEFF

IINNSTTX

– 29 –

How many rectangles are there in the shape below in total?

- 30 -

Take a look at the 12 cups on this page. Two of them are not like all the others. Which are the odd ones out?

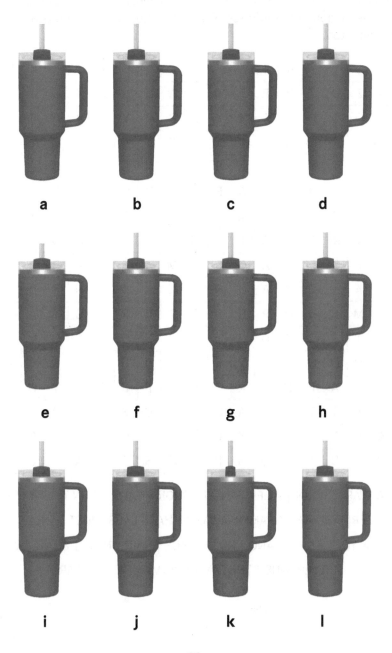

– 31 –

The theme of this word search is one of the world's biggest stars. An Oscar-winning pop singer, and an Oscar-nominated actress, all 15 of the words and phrases hidden in this puzzle are clues to her identity—and her name is hidden in the grid too. Can you figure out who she is and find her name too?

K	U	T	Y	N	E	W	Y	O	R	K	C	I	T	Y	R	H
B	Z	D	Y	R	E	T	W	J	W	U	N	E	Y	D	A	T
I	O	O	R	Y	A	Y	X	O	R	O	Y	G	B	D	E	G
M	F	R	R	A	I	I	L	X	E	J	A	I	J	H	Y	J
H	R	I	N	Y	W	L	N	W	J	M	L	T	U	O	E	A
S	Z	I	N	T	A	A	E	O	E	V	G	Y	S	R	H	G
O	P	P	P	H	H	M	Y	R	N	Y	Z	D	T	R	T	A
N	M	M	S	H	A	I	I	M	X	M	R	U	D	O	F	G
A	E	K	P	F	A	C	S	P	M	W	E	I	A	R	O	Y
I	A	J	E	Q	A	U	N	W	N	A	D	H	N	S	N	D
P	M	H	D	N	P	S	S	G	A	R	R	J	C	T	A	A
K	T	Z	C	S	D	N	V	L	Q	Y	O	G	E	O	M	L
E	N	O	H	P	E	L	E	T	A	V	G	S	Y	R	O	F
E	C	A	F	R	E	K	O	P	I	B	B	E	L	Y	W	L
U	A	T	T	O	N	A	M	R	E	G	S	V	B	B	E	U
A	R	P	N	V	N	Y	O	D	Z	V	Q	G	E	I	S	L
N	B	D	T	Y	Q	N	R	O	B	S	I	R	A	T	S	A

A STAR IS BORN | AMERICAN / HORROR STORY | BORN THIS WAY | GERMANOTTA | GRAMMY AWARD | HAUS LABS | JUST DANCE | NEW YORK CITY | PIANO | POKER FACE | RAIN ON ME | SHALLOW | TELEPHONE | THE FAME | WOMAN OF THE YEAR

Actress _____

– 32 –

Fill in the grid below so that each row of nine squares, each column of nine squares, and each smaller 3 x 3 set of nine squares contain the digits 1-9 once and only once.

There can be no duplicate digits in any row, column, or smaller square.

Can you complete the grid correctly?

1	4		9		5	3	6	2
6	2	9	1	4	3			
5	3		2					4
	5	4				6	8	1
		6	7			2	3	
3			8	1		4		
9	7	3	4	8			2	
	6		5	2	7	8	9	3
2	8		6			1		

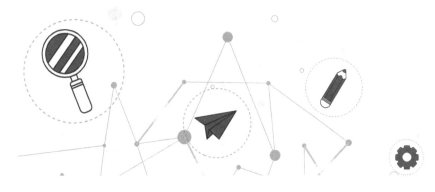

– 33 –

Can you find your way through this maze from one side to the other?

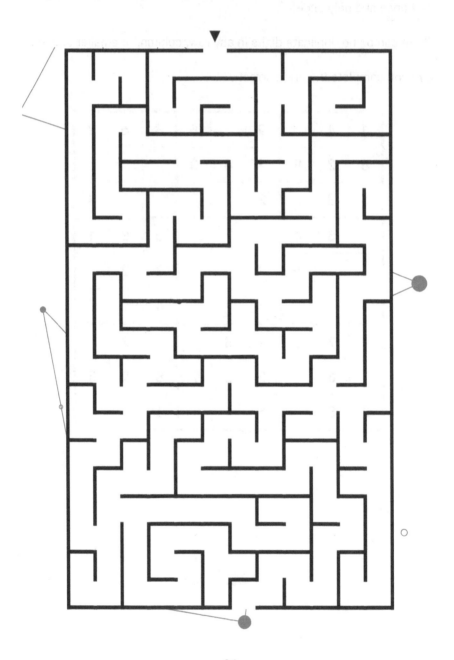

- 34 -

Using only the letters in the box below, can you come up with one 7-letter word, two 6-letter words, three 5-letter words, and four 4-letter words?

E R P S C T E

7 Letters   _ _ _ _ _ _ _

6 Letters   _ _ _ _ _ _   _ _ _ _ _ _

5 Letters   _ _ _ _ _   _ _ _ _ _   _ _ _ _ _

4 Letters   _ _ _ _   _ _ _ _

                    _ _ _ _   _ _ _ _

– 35 –

We're off to history class for this crisscross puzzle. All the words and phrases listed here connect together in the grid. Can you find the right home for each one?

- ABRAHAM LINCOLN
- ANCIENT EGYPT
- BOSTON TEA PARTY
- CIVIL WAR
- CLEOPATRA
- COLUMBUS
- D-DAY
- IWO JIMA
- JOHNSON
- LEE
- MARCO POLO
- MRS. O'LEARY
- PERSIA
- SALEM
- VALKYRIES
- VIETNAM
- WALL STREET CRASH
- WORLD WAR

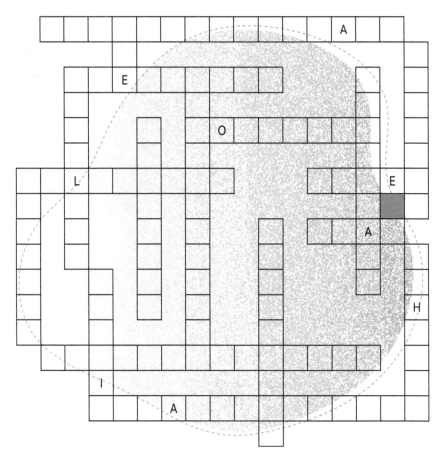

– 36 –

Listed on the left here are the names of eight items of clothing and jewelry. Listed on the right, are the eight places on your body where you would wear them. Can you match them together? The first answer has been filled in for you to make a start.

Stiletto	Head
Cloche	Legs
Alice band	Foot
Bracelet	Finger
Culottes	Hair
Ring	Trunk
Choker	Neck
Corset	Wrist

(Stiletto — Foot)

– 37 –

Three 5-letter words—all the names of dances—have been jumbled together here. Can you piece them back together from the letters provided?

_ _ _ _ A   _ _ _ _ A   _ _ _ _ A

AAAABKLL
MOPRSSU

- 38 -

Each of the 4-letter words in the grid below is missing a letter. If you replace each one correctly, the 6-letter name of a cosmetic will be spelled out down the central column. Watch out, though—there might be multiple possible answers for some of these words, so you'll have to make sure you pick the right one!

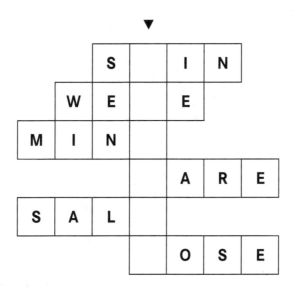

– 39 –

Look at this jumble of hair grips! How many are there on this page?

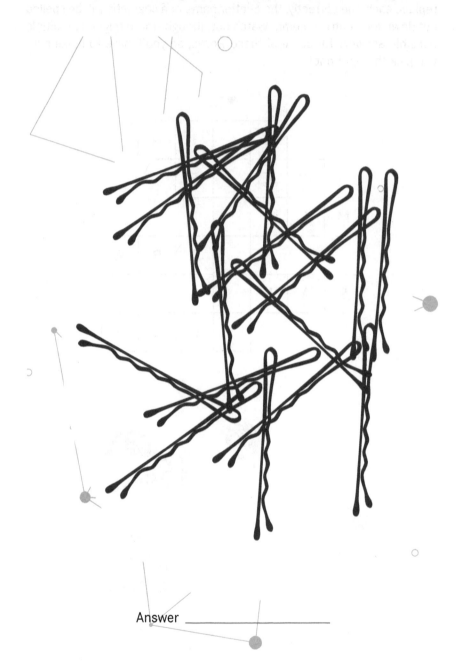

Answer _____

– 40 –

Place the 5-letter answers to the trivia questions below into the corresponding rows in the grid. Once complete, the name of a classic toy for girls will be spelled out down the shaded column.

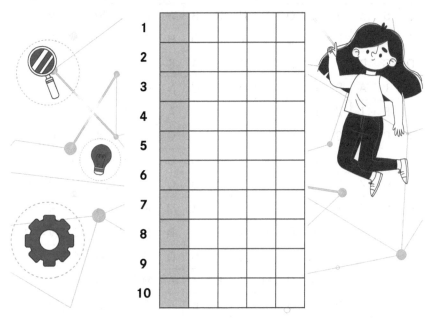

1. What famous religious text is divided into an Old Testament and a New Testament?
2. In math, what can be acute, reflex, or obtuse?
3. What is the first name of the legendary tennis star Federer?
4. What kind of dense, ring-shaped bread roll is uniquely made by boiling the dough in water before baking?
5. In what Asian country was chess invented?
6. Cairo is the capital of what African country?
7. What word can follow San in the name of a Californian city, and precede Luna in the name of a famous Mexican actor?
8. Which legendary television host and journalist (*first name only*) founded the lifestyle magazine *O*?
9. What language did the Ancient Romans speak?
10. What is the first name of the One Direction singer Tomlinson?

- 41 -

Let's take a look at your horoscope for this word search puzzle.

T	I	N	B	P	T	I	N	I	M	E	G	B	C	P	G	Z
S	S	K	J	N	O	S	N	R	B	W	L	C	W	E	M	C
C	E	U	F	C	E	Z	Y	C	O	H	O	B	O	A	G	G
O	G	D	I	C	A	N	D	A	A	S	X	C	P	R	A	U
R	I	A	S	R	T	P	H	T	U	N	O	Z	I	E	G	O
P	F	I	Z	K	A	U	R	I	Z	A	C	Y	O	O	K	Z
I	P	I	G	M	H	U	R	I	A	O	L	E	X	C	C	Q
O	I	H	A	E	I	A	Q	S	C	G	D	B	R	Q	S	Q
A	H	Z	E	R	T	S	T	A	U	O	L	I	U	Y	V	R
U	R	G	Y	T	B	R	U	W	Z	M	R	U	A	M	K	B
G	Z	I	I	X	O	I	V	R	C	B	R	N	E	C	V	O
Z	P	G	E	L	P	C	L	H	U	Q	H	U	O	E	L	F
A	A	T	O	S	O	M	Y	E	Z	A	M	Z	G	C	H	S
S	I	G	P	F	S	I	T	I	B	A	T	Z	R	Y	B	J
B	Y	R	E	Y	K	D	P	M	A	X	Y	H	I	K	Z	P
B	C	W	U	H	O	R	O	S	C	O	P	E	V	T	W	R
M	D	I	U	E	K	W	D	M	E	O	E	A	Z	R	J	X

AQUARIUS | ARIES | ASTROLOGY | CANCER | CAPRICORN | GEMINI |
HOROSCOPE | LEO | LIBRA | PISCES | SAGITTARIUS | SCORPIO |
TAURUS | VIRGO | ZODIAC

− 42 −

Fill in the grid below so that each row of nine squares, each column of nine squares, and each smaller 3 x 3 set of nine squares contain the digits 1-9 once and only once.

There can be no duplicate digits in any row, column, or smaller square.

Can you complete the grid correctly?

8	6	9	1			7		2
1	3				6			9
2		5	3	7	9			1
			4			9	1	
9		8				2	4	3
	7		9		1			5
7		6	8		3	1	2	
		1	6	9				8
	8		7			5	9	6

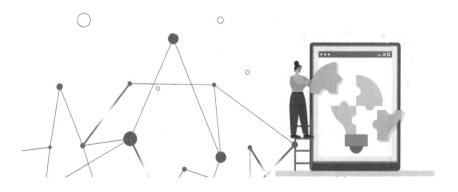

– 43 –

Can you find your way through this maze from one side to the other?

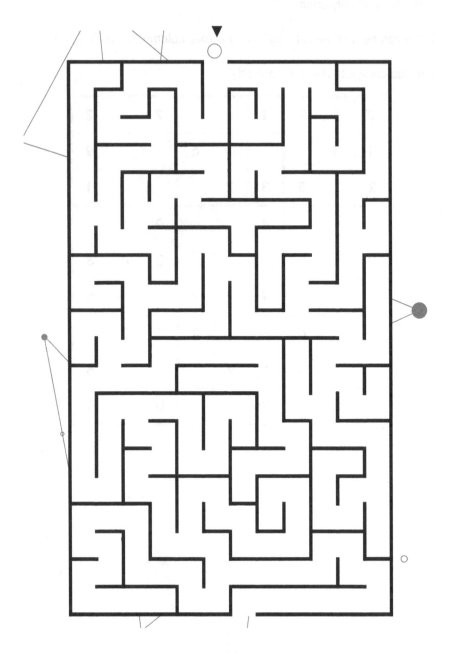

– 44 –

Here's another spiral crossword. Every answer here begins in the corresponding numbered square—but the last letter of one answer becomes the first letter of the next, so that the entire crossword links together like a snake!

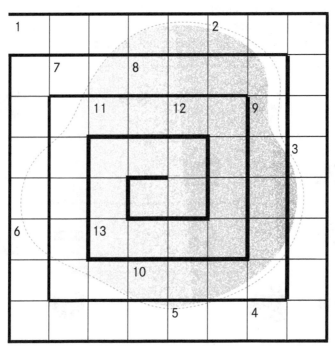

1. Country south of the USA
2. Second color of the rainbow
3. First name of the writer Hemingway
4. Number in a pair
5. *Challengers* star Josh
6. World's largest country
7. Upper limb
8. Stone worker
9. Autumn month
10. Aid organization
11. Title of a knight
12. Hollywood A-lister Ryan
13. Star sign of someone born on Halloween

– 45 –

Here's a tricky play on a standard sudoku game for you—this is a picturedoku!

Can you complete the picture grid below so that no image—a pair of headphones, a pair of sunglasses, a gift, a clapperboard, a bouquet of flowers and a heart—appears more than once in each row of six cells, each column of six cells, and each smaller 3x2 set of six cells?

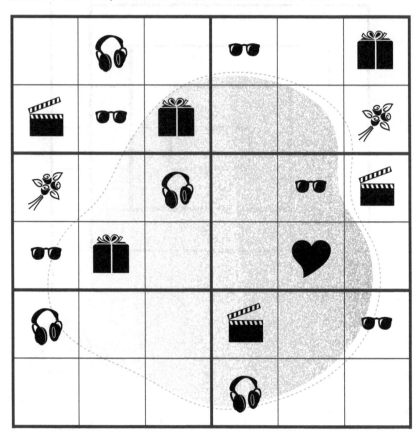

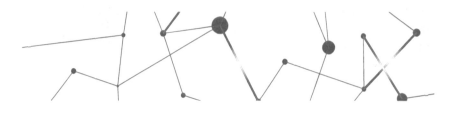

– 46 –

Uh oh, you've misplaced your best make-up brush! Which of these lines—A, B, or C—will lead you to it?

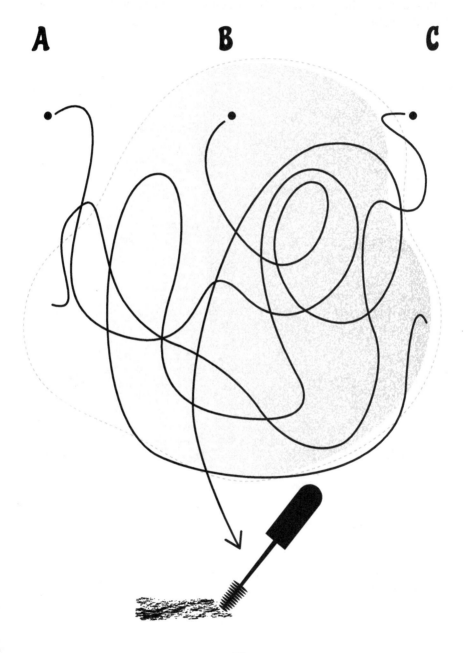

– 47 –

Listed on the left here are the names of eight famous monuments and tourist destinations. On the right are the cities in which they are found. Can you match them together? The first answer has been filled in for you to make a start.

Eiffel Tower	Philadelphia
Acropolis	New York
Liberty Bell	Paris
Space Needle	Pisa
Statue of Liberty	Athens
Buckingham Palace	Rome
Sistine Chapel	London
Leaning Tower	Seattle

– 48 –

The theme of this puzzle is birdlife. The names of 14 birds are hidden in this grid—but they're not in straight lines! They can connect horizontally or vertically, and in any direction, backwards or forwards, upwards or downwards, but never diagonally.

Can you find all the answers, so that no letters are used more than once and there are no unused letters left over? The first answer has been filled in for you to make a start.

W	O	O	D	P	K	K	A	B	U
E	C	K	O	E	O	O	A	R	R
A	U	C	O	C	K	E	R	F	L
G	L	E	T	O	U	L	O	M	A
P	E	R	E	G	C	N	O	I	O
P	E	C	A	R	A	E	G	N	G
I	L	L	R	I	N	P	R	E	T
C	A	A	D	N	S	I	G	I	R
N	N	N	I	E	T	K	E	V	E
O	C	L	A	F	O	R	O	N	O

– 49 –

Let's get baking! Fifteen of the ingredients you might need to bake a cake are hidden in the grid below. Can you track them down and get a sweet treat in the oven?

O	K	H	B	Z	T	X	M	I	B	S	P	A	V	D	S	J
W	B	X	X	Z	O	E	I	B	A	B	M	P	F	G	E	Y
W	I	U	X	T	R	D	D	L	U	X	R	M	G	U	O	W
B	U	A	B	I	Q	Y	L	T	F	H	D	K	A	O	H	H
M	X	M	N	F	I	I	T	G	Z	T	B	Y	D	S	W	I
M	Z	G	L	N	N	E	N	S	G	G	E	C	O	W	M	P
R	U	O	E	A	R	I	E	B	B	S	O	K	S	W	N	P
E	U	E	V	T	T	C	M	S	C	C	J	B	G	S	X	I
R	G	O	W	S	D	L	I	O	O	N	W	Y	N	A	C	N
P	K	O	O	F	E	F	L	A	Q	R	L	E	I	L	I	G
M	Y	R	C	M	T	O	R	F	I	E	R	B	K	T	M	C
F	F	T	A	E	R	Z	J	T	U	W	O	U	A	I	C	R
H	N	R	R	I	A	A	S	I	N	J	K	D	B	P	S	E
W	A	Q	N	A	G	L	C	C	G	F	Z	I	N	E	Y	A
C	P	G	V	M	O	V	H	U	D	T	C	U	O	P	R	M
F	B	A	K	I	N	G	P	O	W	D	E	R	T	U	U	A
Z	J	E	W	N	L	D	T	U	F	A	K	Q	N	Q	P	C

BAKING POWDER | BAKING SODA | BUTTER | CARAMEL | COCOA | COLORING | EGGS | FLOUR | FROSTING | MERINGUE | SALT | SIFTER | SYRUP | VANILLA | WHIPPING CREAM

− 50 −

Fill in the grid below so that each row of nine squares, each column of nine squares, and each smaller 3 x 3 set of nine squares contain the digits 1-9 once and only once.

There can be no duplicate digits in any row, column, or smaller square.

Can you complete the grid correctly?

2	7	8		3	1			9
			9					3
4		9		5	6	7	1	
7			1					4
		2	5			1	9	
1	9	6	3	4		8	7	
			7		5	9	3	
		3	8	1		5	6	7
			6			8		

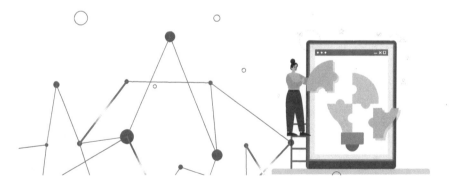

– 51 –

How can you solve this crossword?

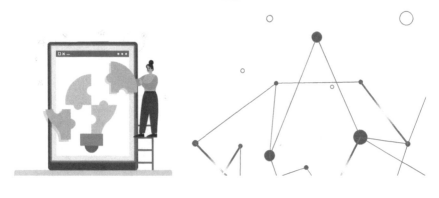

ACROSS

1. Wife's partner
5. Book of maps
8. Using clear, rational thinking
9. Bird's claw
10. Measures of 3ft
11. Receives, takes
12. Careless, slapdash
14. School marks
17. Halloween's month
19. Purplish flower
22. Talent
23. Largest possible
24. Stinks
25. Helps

DOWN

1. Prickly Christmas plant
2. Sweetener for a drink
3. Alleged someone committed a crime
4. American currency
5. Loft space
6. Flat floating leaf on a pond
7. Nasal openings that become blocked when you have a cold
12. Someone who promises money if you complete an action
13. Summary; outer skeleton of a drawing
15. Chills out
16. Ukrainian peninsula annexed by Russia
18. Large male cows
20. Arms and legs
21. Stays in a tent

– 52 –

Can you find your way through this maze from one side to the other?

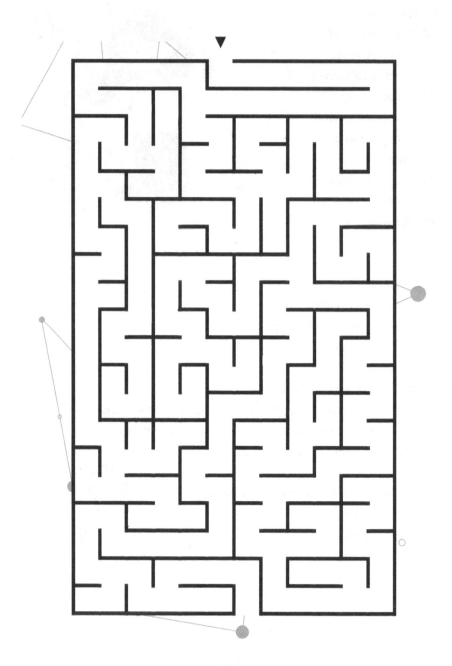

− 53 −

Four friends—Sandy, Candy, Cindy, and Lindy—are walking their dogs in the park. The dogs' names are Rex, Timmy, Rover, and Hector. One of them is a terrier; another is a chihuahua; a third is a labrador; and the fourth is a dachshund. Based on the clues below, can you figure out who owns which dog, and what kind of dog it is?

1. The dachshund is not named Timmy.
2. Rex is the Labrador. His owner isn't Candy.
3. Sandy's dog Hector is a chihuahua.
4. Lindy's dog—which is a terrier—has a 5-letter name.

FRIEND	DOG	BREED
Sandy		
Candy		
Cindy		
Lindy		

− 54 −

Using only the letters below, can you come up with one 7-letter word, two 6-letter words, three 5-letter words, and four 4-letter words?

TRALTES

7 Letters _ _ _ _ _ _ _

6 Letters _ _ _ _ _ _   _ _ _ _ _ _

5 Letters _ _ _ _ _   _ _ _ _ _   _ _ _ _ _

4 Letters _ _ _ _   _ _ _ _

_ _ _ _   _ _ _ _

– 55 –

We're off to the beach for this puzzle! All these words relating to a beach trip connect together in the grid. Can you find the right home for each one?

BOOK	PICNIC	SUNTAN
CAP	SANDALS	SURFBOARD
COOLER	SEA	SWIMMING
DUNES	SEASIDE	TENT
ICE CREAM PARLOR	SNACKS	TOWELS
JETTY	SNORKELING	WATER
PARASOL	SUNBATHE	WINDBREAK
	SUNGLASSES	

– 56 –

Oops! Someone's dropped all the colored pencils on the desk! How many are there to pick up?

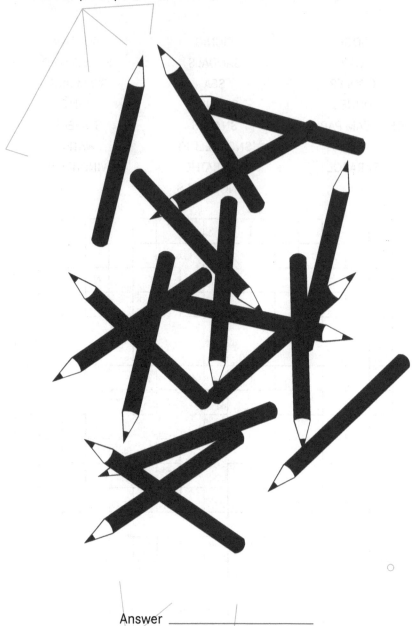

Answer _____

– 57 –

In this crossword, all the answers are anagrams of the clue words. Can you solve them all?

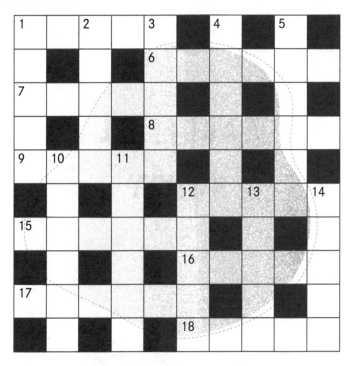

ACROSS 1. STOAT | **6.** MANILA | **7.** MALER | **8.** GREENY | **9.** DEISM | **12.** BEARS | **15.** AMUSES | **16.** TACIT | **17.** LEADER | **18.** STUDS.

DOWN 1. TRIED | **2.** MALAR | **3.** MATES | **4.** ANEMIC | **5.** ANGLED | **10.** DISUSE | **11.** SQUEAL | **12.** BARED | **13.** TEARS | **14.** CASKS.

– 58 –

Three 5-letter words—all the names of different sweet treats—have been jumbled together below. Can you unscramble them?

_ _ _ _Y   _ _ _ _Y   _ _ _ _Y

AACDFFLLL
NOTYYY

– 59 –

Each of the sentences below contain a part of the body hidden somewhere between the words. Can you find them all? The first has been highlighted for you to make a start...

1

"Can you **hear** that?"

Heart

_____

2

"They're emus! Clever birds, too!"

_____

3

"We should err on the side of caution..."

_____

4

"It's the quaintest in every way!"

_____

5

"The scientist creates all sorts of things—from robots to machines."

_____

63

− 60 −

Place the 7-letter answers to the trivia questions below into the corresponding rows in the grid. Once complete, the name of a classic fairy tale will be spelled out down the shaded column.

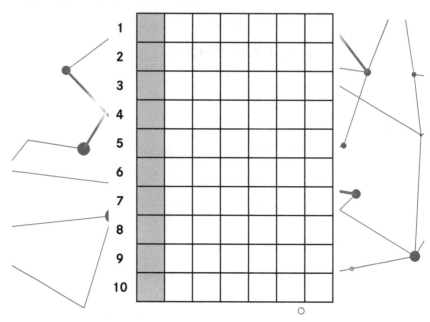

1. What word can mean the main city in a country and an uppercase letter?
2. In what language does arrivederci mean goodbye?
3. What kind of power station might suffer a meltdown?
4. What precious stone is also the hardest natural mineral in the world?
5. What short, straight hair found on the upper part of the face is also known as a cilium?
6. What was Adele doing In the Deep in the title of a 2011 hit?
7. What was the name of Franklin D. Roosevelt's wife, who served as his First Lady from 1933 until 1945?
8. What is the surname of *Friends* actor Matt, who played the part of Joey in the long-running series?
9. What are paired with Chutes in the title of a simple dice-rolling board game?
10. Florida shares a land border with Georgia and which other US state?

- 61 -

Here's a word search—with a fiendish twist! Hidden in this book are the names of 15 Hollywood actors and actresses. To find them, though, you're going to have to first work out their names, from which all of the vowels have been removed! Can you figure out the names, and then track them down in the grid?

K	C	O	L	L	U	B	A	R	D	N	A	S	K	N	G	C
F	H	T	R	O	W	S	M	E	H	S	I	R	H	C	D	Q
J	A	K	E	G	Y	L	L	E	N	H	A	A	L	N	N	H
S	Z	U	E	K	O	O	T	K	A	B	L	U	J	I	A	U
C	D	X	N	H	M	T	F	N	H	X	G	U	P	A	T	G
M	U	L	V	T	L	N	P	J	W	C	L	L	A	T	A	H
T	E	G	O	K	N	F	U	W	G	I	M	U	N	S	L	J
N	N	R	J	N	G	A	L	G	A	D	O	T	N	A	I	A
U	I	W	Y	O	Y	O	E	R	Q	Q	X	A	E	H	E	C
L	P	F	Q	L	B	E	O	X	Z	K	V	M	H	C	P	K
B	S	J	Z	X	S	B	R	S	N	E	L	F	A	A	O	M
Y	I	K	Z	L	E	T	J	N	S	O	M	G	T	C	R	A
L	R	X	Y	R	D	Y	R	I	A	D	A	Z	H	I	T	N
I	H	R	T	F	S	W	R	E	P	Y	E	X	A	S	M	W
M	C	S	N	O	W	H	B	H	E	I	R	W	W	S	A	M
E	L	I	B	B	C	E	K	Y	X	P	H	X	A	E	N	I
U	J	C	H	R	I	S	P	R	A	T	T	I	Y	J	X	A

_NN_H_TH_W_Y | CHR_S _V_NS | CHR_S H_MSW_RTH | CHR_S P_N_ |
CHR_S PR_TT | _M_LY BL_NT | G_L G_D_T | H_GH J_CKM_N |
J_K_ GYLL_NH__L | J_SS_C_ CH_ST__N | J_L__ R_B_RTS |
M_RYL STR__P | N_T_L__ P_RTM_N | RY_N R_YN_LDS |
S_NDR_ B_LL_CK

– 62 –

Fill in the grid below so that each row of nine squares, each column of nine squares, and each smaller 3 x 3 set of nine squares contain the digits 1-9 once and only once.

There can be no duplicate digits in any row, column, or smaller square.

Can you complete the grid correctly?

	2				5			7
1	9			6	2	4	3	5
				1	9	6		
7		8					6	4
						2		
9	5			4	6		8	
3	6	1	9			8	4	
4		5		2	1			
2	7	9	6	8	4	3		

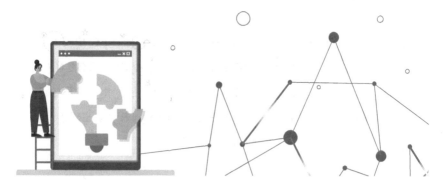

– 63 –

Can you find your way through this maze from one side to the other?

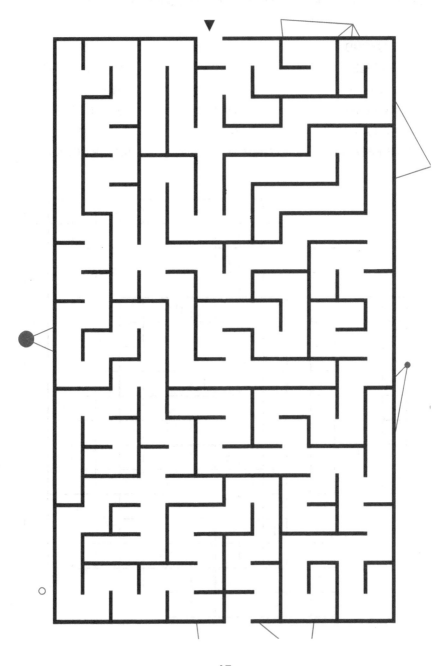

- 64 -

Who wants a cookie? All these cookie types and ingredients connect together in the grid below. Can you find the right home for each one?

ALMOND	HAZELNUT	OREO
APPLE	ICING	PEANUT BUTTER
BUTTER	MACARON	THUMBPRINT
CARAMEL	MINT	SHORTBREAD
CHOCOLATE CHIP	NUT	SNAP
GINGERBREAD	OAT AND RAISIN	SUGAR COOKIES

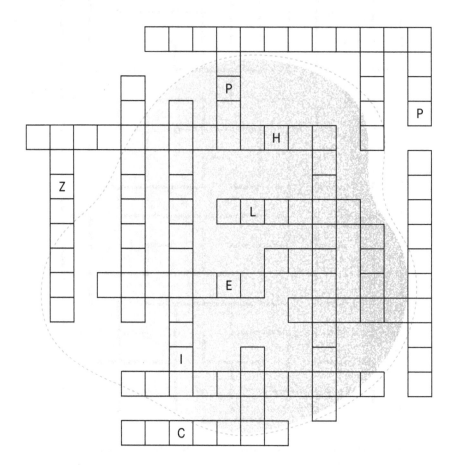

– 65 –

Listed on the left here are the names of eight amazing sportswomen. On the right are their sports. Can you match them together? The first answer has been filled in for you.

Venus Williams	Golf
Simone Biles	Tennis
Megan Rapinoe	Basketball
Nelly Korda	Boxing
Lisa Leslie	Swimming
Sha'Carri Richardson	Soccer
Katie Ledecky	Athletics
Claressa Shields	Gymnastics

(Venus Williams — Tennis)

– 66 –

Here's another spiral crossword. Each answer here begins in the corresponding numbered square—but the last letter of one answer becomes the first letter of the next, so that the entire crossword links together like a snake!

1. At what time?
2. Not in any place
3. Precisely
4. Day before today
5. Not old
6. Impressive, very large
7. Canine animal
8. Coy, high-pitched laugh
9. Completed, stopped
10. Let down
11. Inner digit of the hand
12. Makes lighter, illuminates more

– 67 –

Every letter of the alphabet appears in the grid below at least twice—except two. One letter doesn't appear at all, and one letter appears only once and so does not have a pair. What letters are the odd ones out?

I	P	G	M	F	Q	B
X	C	S	R	K	H	O
F	Z	K	D	A	W	U
Y	O	A	W	Y	S	J
R	T	J	Q	Z	X	G
H	L	U	E	N	C	P
D	E	B	N	I	M	T

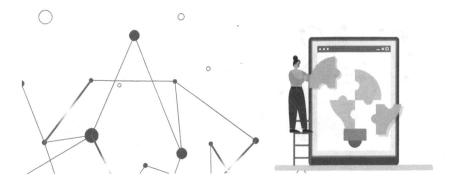

– 68 –

All the vowels have been removed from this simple crossword grid. Can you complete it?

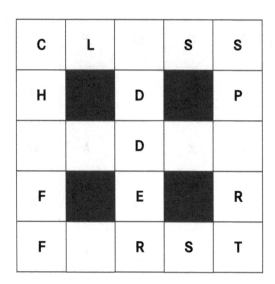

– 69 –

All six of these 6-letter words can be rearranged to spell six new ones. What do those six new words all have in common?

MADDEN   EDITED

TRADED   SHADED

PADDER   INDEED

Answers
_____
_____
_____
_____
_____
_____

– 70 –

Four school friends—Amy, Beatrice, Clara, and Di—are discussing the marks they got on four end-of-term tests. The four marks they're discussing are an A+, an A−, a C, and a D. Each test was in a different subject: history, math, geography, and science. Based on the clues below, can you work out which friend scored what mark, and in which subject they achieved it?

1. The D mark was scored on a very hard geography test!

2. Di scored an A− in a subject ending in a letter Y.

3. Beatrice is the science whizz of the group and scored a deserved A+ on her test!

4. Amy did not score a C grade.

	A+	A−	C	D	History	Math	Geography	Science
Amy								
Beatrice								
Clara								
Di								
History								
Math								
Geography								
Science								

FRIEND	MARK	SUBJECT
Amy		
Beatrice		
Clara		
Di		

– 71 –

Here's an EX-cellent test of your wordpower—in the guise of a word search!

The answers to the 15 clues below are all 9-letter words that begin with the letters EX-. Those words are all hidden in the grid. Can you solve the clues and find the answers?

P	J	O	C	D	E	X	T	R	A	C	T	E	D	G	G	U
V	S	D	Z	W	E	X	A	L	O	J	R	E	M	C	G	S
R	U	E	X	K	V	S	Y	E	L	I	X	Z	E	N	J	A
D	E	U	T	S	N	S	I	Q	X	P	E	E	I	S	K	E
I	L	X	A	A	W	Z	E	C	L	Q	X	D	Q	W	X	A
M	D	O	A	E	V	Z	R	O	R	H	N	L	H	P	N	B
E	M	E	K	M	V	A	S	Q	A	E	C	W	L	E	S	I
X	I	F	G	O	I	I	C	U	T	G	X	A	L	P	Q	O
C	E	J	C	N	V	N	S	X	P	U	I	E	Z	G	J	E
E	X	L	K	E	A	T	E	S	E	N	Y	R	N	P	T	F
L	C	K	W	O	E	H	R	R	E	R	I	I	C	A	K	D
L	L	Z	M	D	B	W	C	D	S	C	L	X	I	V	G	O
E	U	X	L	D	S	E	R	X	T	L	X	L	R	H	D	H
N	D	N	U	C	G	X	G	W	E	R	O	E	F	S	S	R
T	I	U	K	K	X	A	F	P	J	F	K	X	U	D	U	M
K	N	X	Z	P	M	U	X	N	X	M	D	H	I	G	H	T
Y	G	R	L	J	B	E	L	E	X	C	L	A	I	M	E	D

1. People who carry out school tests | 2. Digs out of the ground | 3. Brilliant | 4. Disproportionate, more than is necessary | 5. Swapped | 6. Said out loud | 7. Ignoring, missing out | 8. Worked out physically | 9. Cleanse the skin | 10. Very tired | 11. Throwing out of school | 12. Made clear to someone | 13. Capable of blowing up | 14. Making longer | 15. Removed, took out.

- 72 -

How quickly can you solve this crossword?

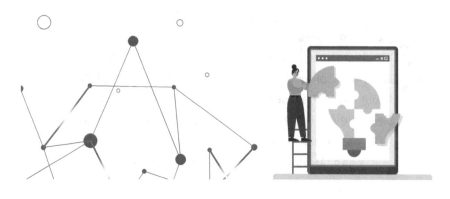

ACROSS

1. Incline
4. Exclusive news story
10. Give a better job to
11. Precise
12. Danger
13. Rising to your feet
15. Wonderful, glorious
19. Group of ferocious wild canine animals
20. Masculine
23. Mushrooms
24. Tidal wave
25. Droopy
26. Ascend, go up a mountain

DOWN

2. Rings, circles
3. End-of-term party
5. Type of T-shirt with a rounded collar
6. Audience's standing tribute to a performance
7. Flicker, glimmer
8. Diploma, document showing an achievement
9. Where an actor performs
14. Cutting, trimming
16. Capital of Georgia
17. Fast
18. Satan
21. Siren
22. Drag, haul

– 73 –

Fill in the grid below so that each row of nine squares, each column of nine squares, and each smaller 3 x 3 set of nine squares contain the digits 1-9 once and only once.

There can be no duplicate digits in any row, column, or smaller square.

Can you complete the grid correctly?

		7		2		3	4	
		8	4	7	9		1	5
1	5					9		
7	8			4	2	1		
		9			7		2	4
4	2		6	5		8	9	7
		2						
9			2	8	5	7	6	
5	7			3				9

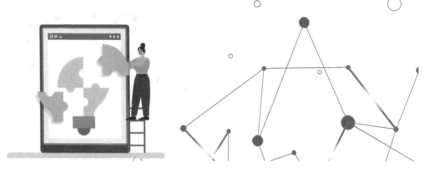

– 76 –

Two 7-letter words—both the names of pasta—have been jumbled together here. Can you unjumble them?

L _ _ _ _ _ _   _ _ _ _ L _ _

AAAFGII
LLLNSSU

– 77 –

What 4-word phrase has been coded into the image below?

SAIL

SEA SEA SEA   SEA SEA SEA

SEA

Answer _____

– 78 –

We're rummaging through the wardrobe for this crisscross puzzle. All of these clothing-related words connect together in the grid. Can you find the right home for each one?

BATHING COSTUME	COAT	OVERALL
BIKINI	DART	PLAID
BLAZER	DRESS	PULLOVER
BLOUSE	HEM	SNEAKERS
BOOTS	HORIZONTAL STRIPE	SUSPENDERS
BRACELET	MITTENS	TIE
CARDIGAN	NECKLINE	TURTLENECK

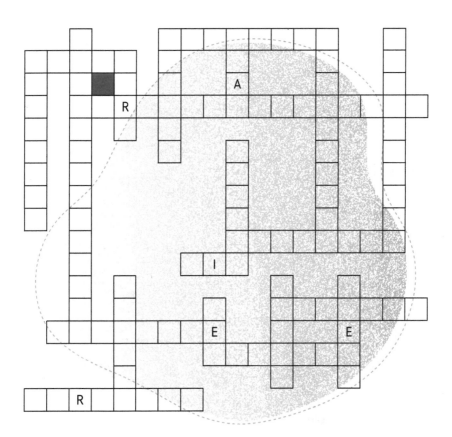

– 79 –

Using only the letters below, can you come up with one 7-letter word, two 6-letter words, three 5-letter words, and four 4-letter words?

S E J R T E C

7 Letters _ _ _ _ _ _ _

6 Letters _ _ _ _ _ _   _ _ _ _ _ _

5 Letters _ _ _ _ _   _ _ _ _ _   _ _ _ _ _

4 Letters _ _ _ _   _ _ _ _

_ _ _ _   _ _ _ _

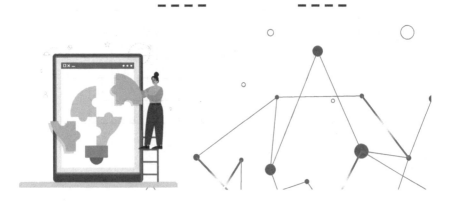

– 80 –

Place the 5-letter answers to the trivia questions below into the corresponding rows in the grid. Once complete, the name of a hit song by Taylor Swift will be spelled out down the shaded column.

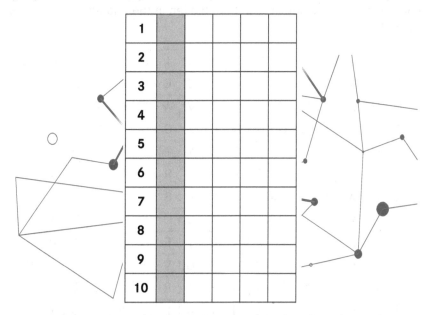

1. What Colonial Massachusetts village was the location of an infamous series of witch trials in the 1690s?
2. What organ of the body would be examined by a specialist called a cardiologist?
3. What word for a grand sports stadium or events space—which begins and ends with the same letter—takes its name from the Latin word for sand?
4. What Australian mammal is known for its diet of eucalyptus leaves and sleeping up to 22 hours a day?
5. How many musicians would perform in an octet?
6. In what Asian country is the port of Goa located?
7. In what US state did the famous Battle of the Alamo take place?
8. By what man's name is a movie industry Academy Award better known?
9. 20% is the equivalent of what fraction?
10. Who did Elijah Wood play in the *Lord of the Rings* movies?

- 81 -

We're off around the world for this word search, with this list of famous cities and holiday destinations. But this puzzle has a twist—as well as finding the names of all 10 of these places in the grid, the names of the countries in which they're found are hidden in the grid as well. Can you track down all 24 answers?

K	V	M	A	N	E	D	E	W	S	I	R	W	E	O	K	S
B	wB	X	O	B	T	F	H	F	S	E	L	H	S	Z	L	O
R	H	R	L	D	U	G	M	T	V	W	B	G	T	A	Q	R
A	V	T	R	Q	G	C	A	U	S	C	H	I	N	A	A	I
Z	O	M	M	R	J	N	O	C	N	I	L	B	U	D	C	E
I	B	H	G	Z	B	C	I	M	S	R	Z	U	H	Y	J	N
L	A	A	B	U	N	P	L	K	L	S	R	R	O	I	S	A
Q	D	V	L	A	N	V	O	W	D	O	Y	P	J	H	I	J
A	A	A	V	D	L	X	N	U	J	E	H	D	I	J	R	E
T	N	N	S	Q	I	O	D	Z	G	V	T	K	N	A	A	D
H	A	A	H	N	F	N	O	Y	T	R	H	I	C	E	P	O
E	C	N	A	R	F	Z	N	I	A	L	E	B	N	O	Y	I
N	W	T	N	A	I	R	O	B	I	O	E	E	Z	U	T	R
S	L	V	G	A	I	L	A	R	T	S	U	A	C	R	Y	S
I	E	I	H	G	Z	G	M	P	A	Y	N	E	K	E	Q	I
H	X	W	A	Z	B	C	D	N	A	L	E	R	I	S	D	E
R	P	K	I	I	Y	T	U	R	K	E	Y	I	U	Y	W	P

ATHENS _____ | DUBLIN _____

HAVANA _____ | ISTANBUL _____ | LONDON _____

NAIROBI _____ | PARIS _____ | RIO DE JANEIRO _____

SHANGHAI _____ STOCKHOLM _____ | SYDNEY _____

VANCOUVER _____

– 82 –

Fill in the grid below so that each row of nine squares, each column of nine squares, and each smaller 3 x 3 set of nine squares contain the digits 1-9 once and only once.

There can be no duplicate digits in any row, column, or smaller square.

Can you complete the grid correctly?

5	3			6		1	9	
	2	1						6
6		9	1	2	3			
2		5			7	6		
8	4		6			9	7	
7					9		2	4
		2			5			7
1	8		2		6	4	5	9
		4			1			

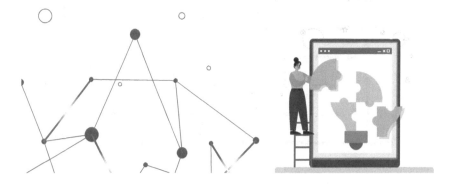

– 83 –

Can you find your way through this maze from one side to the other?

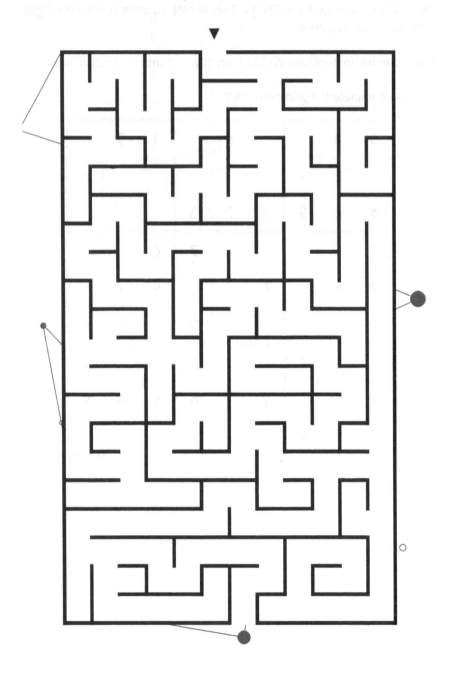

– 84 –

Listed on the left here are the names of eight best-selling musical artists. On the right, are the names of eight albums they released in the 2020s. Can you match them together? The first answer has been filled in for you to make a start.

Katy Perry — Smile

Adele

The Weeknd

Taylor Swift

Beyoncé

Ariana Grande

Olivia Rodrigo

SZA

Guts

SOS

Smile

After Hours

Eternal Sunshine

Midnights

30

Cowboy Carter

− 85 −

Each of the 4-letter words in the grid below is missing a letter. If you replace each one correctly, a 6-letter cartoon character will be spelled out down the central column. Watch out, thought—there might be multiple possible answers for some of these words, so you'll have to make sure you pick the right one!

– 86 –

In this crossword, all the answers in the grid are anagrams of the clue words below.

ACROSS 1. FEARS | **4.** WEST | **7.** STOPS | **8.** SAGE | **9.** NORTH | **11.** RAISE | **15.** GEAR | **16.** CANED | **17.** STAB | **18.** BORES.

DOWN 1. PURSE | **2.** FATS | **3.** SISTER | **5.** TIGRE | **6.** SAW | **10.** ADHERE | **12.** GIRTH | **13.** REEFS | **14.** BUNS | **15.** ORB.

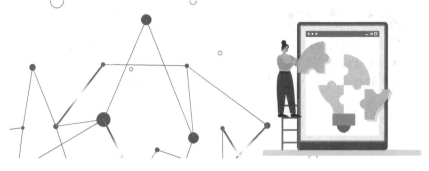

– 87 –

Each answer here begins in the corresponding numbered square—but the last letter of one answer becomes the first letter of the next, so that the entire crossword links together like a snake!

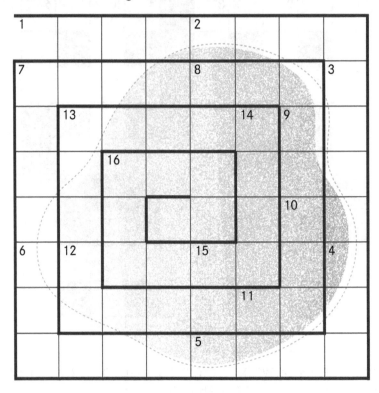

1. Shade, hue
2. Correct
3. In that place
4. Spring festival
5. Thieves, burglars
6. Look at intensely
7. Ahead of time
8. 365 days
9. Decay
10. Not that
11. Grinned
12. Let slip from your hands
13. Oyster's gem
14. In the nearby area
15. Not heavy
16. On this date, now

– 88 –

Take a look at the 16 cellphones on this page. Two of them are not like all the others. Which are the odd ones out?

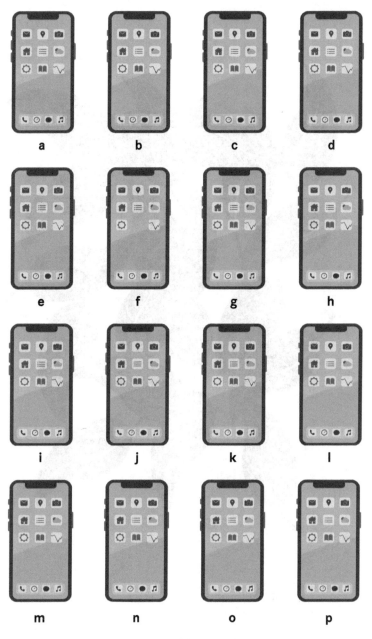

– 89 –

Autumn is coming, and the leaves are starting to fall... How many have fallen on this page?

Answer _____

− 90 −

There are some very peculiar words hidden in this grid, but all of them have something in common—they're all the name of a kind of something, the name of which is also hidden in the grid. What is the missing answer that connects them all?

M	M	A	I	X	T	G	N	E	H	Z	U	G	P	M	V	E
J	U	H	C	J	A	A	O	S	H	N	G	N	V	B	M	Z
H	A	S	K	I	R	R	D	L	I	B	F	O	I	J	M	X
S	T	C	I	S	D	F	P	M	G	A	D	L	B	I	T	I
B	Y	A	N	C	W	O	E	D	L	E	Q	L	R	R	D	C
B	A	L	P	M	A	R	L	P	Z	C	V	I	A	E	Q	E
V	V	L	K	J	E	L	H	E	L	Y	Y	R	P	H	C	M
C	O	I	Y	H	H	O	I	A	M	D	H	A	H	T	F	B
H	D	O	T	Q	R	M	V	N	R	A	M	C	O	I	N	A
I	E	P	L	N	D	I	U	U	S	A	Z	I	N	Z	N	L
T	C	E	C	O	C	R	G	I	R	T	R	M	E	S	A	O
A	L	X	B	H	L	Y	I	I	N	B	R	E	J	X	N	T
R	Y	R	O	D	D	G	M	Z	T	O	B	U	B	F	V	Q
R	O	R	F	R	N	B	F	S	U	G	H	F	M	E	D	H
A	D	Z	U	M	A	C	N	H	E	S	N	P	J	E	C	X
X	Y	H	D	A	T	I	M	P	A	N	I	Z	U	D	N	G
F	S	H	Z	U	N	W	W	S	Y	X	T	C	I	E	G	T

ALPHORN | CALLIOPE | CARILLON | CEMBALO | CHITARRA | CLAVICHORD | DOBRO | EUPHONIUM | GUZHENG | HURDY-GURDY | MARIMBA | MELODICA | REBEC | THEREMIN | TIMPANI | VIBRAPHONE | ZITHER

HIDDEN ANSWER: _____

- 91 -

How quickly can you solve this puzzle?

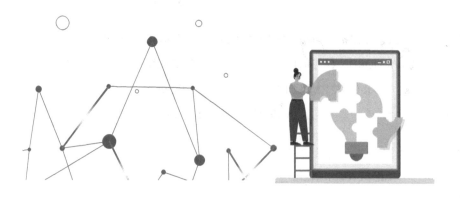

ACROSS

1. Issue, difficulty
5. Tricky puzzle or question; arrogant, self-publicizing person
8. Alterations
9. Made simpler or more relaxed
10. Theatrical work
11. Mound of termite-like creatures
12. Eerie, spooky (two words)
15. Exam scores
17. Musical tones
20. Public square or precinct
21. Adolescent, of young adult age
22. Divide
23. Over-the-shoulder school bag

DOWN

1. Walked, stepped
2. Japanese city
3. Tourist's bags
4. New England state
5. Decorative fabric fold
6. Raw fish dish
7. Warning sign, as in a relationship (two words)
12. Colored bars
13. Download a new program onto a device
14. Most lengthy
16. Smallest quantity
18. Educate
19. Witch's incantation

– 92 –

Fill in the grid below so that each row of nine squares, each column of nine squares, and each smaller 3 x 3 set of nine squares contain the digits 1-9 once and only once.

There can be no duplicate digits in any row, column, or smaller square.

Can you complete the grid correctly?

						6	3	4
6			5	4	1		2	7
	8	7		6	2		9	5
		8		1		9	4	3
							8	1
1				3	8	5		6
7	4		6		5		1	9
8	5		7	9		4		2
		6	1			7		

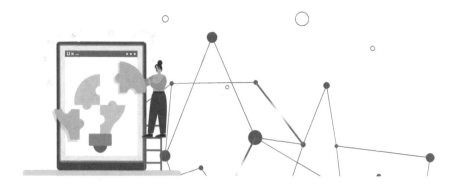

- 93 -

Can you find your way through this maze from one side to the other?

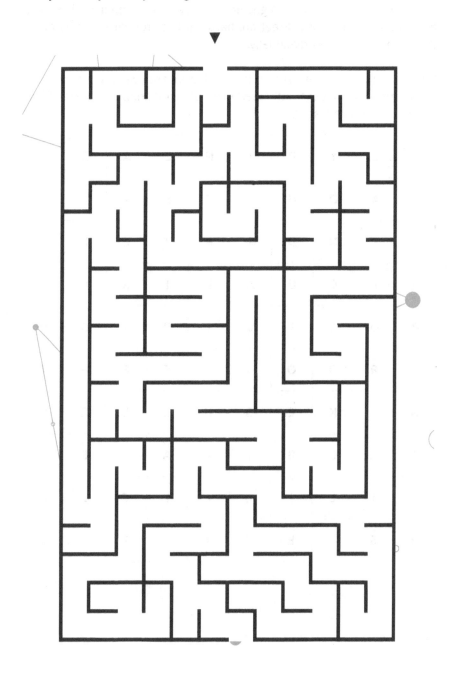

– 94 –

The names of 12 best-selling pop stars of the 2020s are hidden in this grid—but they're not in straight lines! They can connect horizontally or vertically, and in any direction, backwards or forwards, upwards or downwards, but never diagonally.

Can you find all the answers, so that no letters are used more than once and there are no unused letters left over? The first answer has been filled in for you to make a start.

B	E	Y	P	I	N	L	A	D	Y
T	A	O	H	A	K	S	T	Y	G
L	Y	N	D	R	R	Y	E	L	A
O	É	C	U	A	L	I	S	A	G
R	O	L	I	V	I	P	A	C	H
S	R	D	O	R	A	E	P	P	A
W	I	K	E	S	H	L	L	R	O
I	G	O	B	I	A	A	D	E	A
F	T	L	I	L	L	L	E	L	N
H	S	I	E	E	I	I	Z	Z	O

– 95 –

Using only the letters below, can you come up with one 7-letter word, two 6-letter words, three 5-letter words, and four 4-letter words?

TAIRRPO

7 Letters _ _ _ _ _ _ _

6 Letters _ _ _ _ _ _   _ _ _ _ _ _

5 Letters _ _ _ _ _   _ _ _ _ _   _ _ _ _ _

4 Letters _ _ _ _   _ _ _ _

_ _ _ _   _ _ _ _

– 96 –

Listed on the left here are eight somewhat unusual words! On the right are eight much simpler words that have roughly the same meaning. Can you match pairs together? The first answer has been filled in for you to make a start.

Lithe	Maze
Listless	Flexible
Lexicon	Sendup
Labyrinth	Star
Laborious	Weary
Languish	Difficult
Luminary	Vocabulary
Lampoon	Weaken

Lithe — Flexible

– 97 –

Place the 6-letter answers to the trivia questions below into the corresponding rows in the grid on the next page. Once complete, a well-known 5-word phrase will be spelled out down the shaded column.

1. Found in north Africa, what is the world's largest desert?
2. Which sign of the zodiac is represented by a bull?
3. What is the first word in the acronyms US, UK, and UN?
4. What is the capital of the state of South Dakota?
5. What is the first name of the Oscar-nominated actress Staunton, who played the queen in Netflix's *The Crown*, and Dolores Umbrage in the *Harry Potter* movies?
6. In the Old Testament, who removed a thorn from a lion's paw?
7. In what New York city is Cornell University located?
8. What planet in our solar system is famous for its enormous series of rings?
9. What word follows Baltic, States, and Pacific in the names of three Monopoly properties?
10. What is Venus Williams' fellow tennis-playing sister named?
11. What is the first name of the country superstar Twain, whose hit singles include "Waking Up Dreaming" and "Man! I Feel Like a Woman"?
12. How many are there in a dozen?
13. What is the name of the sea witch in Disney's *The Little Mermaid*?
14. One of the infamous places of the Second World War, in what European country is Auschwitz located?
15. What is the opposite of the word 'export', referring to a product that is brought into a country from overseas?
16. What famous film studio, known for children's animated movies, bought fellow animation studio Pixar for over $7 billion in 2006?
17. What word for a young girl is often used in literature to describe a young woman who is 'in distress'?
18. In what US state will you find an NBA team called the Blazers, a WHL team called the Winterhawks, and a Minor League Baseball team called the Hillsboro Hops?
19. What famous American inventor had the first names Thomas Alva?
20. What is the first name of the rock superstar Crow, whose hit singles include All "I Wanna Do" and "If It Makes You Happy"?

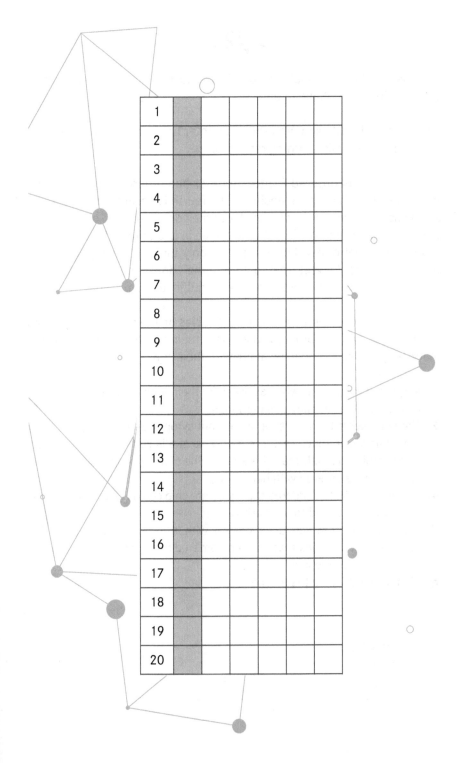

– 98 –

Brace yourself for this final logic puzzle, because here you have not three but four different options to unpick!

A mom, a dad, their son, and their daughter have stopped by the local coffee shop for a mid-morning rest stop.

One of them has ordered a latte; another has ordered a cappuccino; someone else is having a macchiato; the fourth is having a mocha. Each person has requested an extra detail with their drink, too: one of the drinks is to go; another has an extra shot of coffee in it; a third is decaf; and the fourth has a shot of hazelnut syrup. Not only that, but each person has ordered a different sweet treat to go with their drink: added onto the end of the order there is a donut, a cookie, a muffin, and a brownie.

Based on the clues below, and using the tables on the opposite page, can you work out who has ordered what, what their added extra is, and what snack they've decided to have along with their drink?

1. It is one of the parents who has asked for their drink to be decaf. (They've had two coffees already this morning!)
2. The daughter is having a shot of hazelnut syrup added to her latte.
3. Mom has a hair appointment to get to, so she is getting her drink to go and catching up with the others later. She's also taking the chocolate brownie she's ordered with her as well!
4. The person who has ordered the chocolate chip cookie is having an extra shot of coffee added to their drink.
5. The cappuccino—which does not go with the custard donut on the order!—is not the drink that has been ordered to go, nor does it have the extra shot of coffee in it.
6. Mom is not drinking the mocha.

	Latte	Cappuccino	Macchiato	Mocha	To go	Extra shot	Decaf	Hazelnut syrup	Donut	Cookie	Muffin	Brownie
Mom												
Dad												
Son												
Daughter												
Donut												
Cookie												
Muffin												
Brownie												
To go												
Extra shot												
Decaf												
Hazelnut syrup												

PERSON	DRINK	EXTRA	SNACK
Mom			
Dad			
Son			
Daughter			

107

– 99 –

Let's double things up for this final word search, with not one but two letter grids!

Hidden across these two pages are 30 two-word phrases, both of which have eight letters. The first word is hidden in the first grid, and the second from each phrase is hidden in the grid on the opposite page. Can you track down all 60 answers across both grids?

P	T	R	V	A	H	P	E	R	S	O	N	A	L	K	W	S
B	I	R	T	H	D	A	Y	D	E	G	T	G	G	N	L	U
C	O	N	M	P	B	A	E	D	V	N	N	N	N	E	I	R
O	R	Y	P	K	F	T	U	L	I	I	O	I	I	K	A	V
H	B	E	K	O	A	T	M	A	T	D	I	P	K	A	T	I
I	E	E	A	L	I	I	T	A	I	L	T	P	N	T	K	V
G	I	J	O	T	L	N	V	K	S	I	C	O	I	S	C	A
G	V	S	L	I	U	P	T	Q	O	U	E	H	R	I	O	L
L	I	A	T	O	P	R	A	T	P	B	L	S	D	M	C	C
E	Q	A	M	K	O	H	E	R	C	Z	E	Y	A	V	F	O
D	R	P	K	K	R	A	Y	C	A	E	Y	P	O	O	O	M
Y	P	U	N	H	T	J	D	D	O	L	R	T	H	L	R	P
E	G	A	I	R	R	A	M	J	R	V	L	I	Y	C	E	U
P	L	E	G	N	A	H	C	X	E	O	E	E	D	A	N	T
J	Q	L	A	C	I	M	E	H	C	B	G	R	L	N	S	E
I	K	V	U	E	T	E	L	P	M	O	C	E	Y	I	I	R
N	G	N	A	T	I	O	N	A	L	B	Q	C	N	C	C	H

- ALTITUDE / SICKNESS
- BIRTHDAY / PRESENTS
- BUILDING / MATERIAL
- CHEMICAL / COMPOUND
- COCKTAIL / WAITRESS
- COMPLETE / STRANGER
- COMPUTER / KEYBOARD
- CREATURE / COMFORTS
- DRINKING / FOUNTAIN
- ELECTION / CAMPAIGN
- EXCHANGE / STUDENTS
- FORENSIC / MEDICINE
- HIGGLEDY / PIGGLEDY
- HYDROGEN / PEROXIDE

108

- INDIRECT / QUESTION
- ISOLATED / INCIDENT
- MARRIAGE / PROPOSAL
- MILITARY / HOSPITAL
- MISTAKEN / IDENTITY
- MOUNTAIN / CLIMBING
- NATIONAL / MONUMENT
- PARALLEL / UNIVERSE
- PERSONAL / PROPERTY
- PINPOINT / ACCURACY
- PORTRAIT / PAINTING
- POSITIVE / THINKING
- RECOVERY / POSITION
- SHOPPING / PRECINCT
- SURVIVAL / INSTINCT
- VOLCANIC / ERUPTION

D	F	G	M	U	D	R	T	G	N	I	B	M	I	L	C	Z
S	T	N	E	D	U	T	S	N	T	C	N	I	C	E	R	P
J	R	E	G	N	A	R	T	S	E	A	S	O	V	M	P	P
M	H	C	O	M	F	O	R	T	S	M	M	Q	Y	A	R	I
H	Q	M	A	T	E	R	I	A	L	P	U	D	I	O	S	Y
H	P	O	S	I	T	I	O	N	O	H	E	N	P	Q	T	J
V	G	K	L	J	N	G	T	U	C	L	T	E	O	I	N	P
Y	K	O	L	W	I	P	N	C	G	I	R	M	T	E	E	E
C	E	G	A	L	A	D	O	G	N	T	D	N	B	R	S	N
A	Y	N	S	A	T	I	I	G	Y	I	E	E	O	F	E	I
R	B	I	O	T	N	P	T	N	S	D	T	X	N	S	R	C
U	O	K	P	I	U	T	S	R	I	M	I	S	R	T	P	I
C	A	N	O	P	O	X	E	G	E	D	Z	E	N	A	W	D
C	R	I	R	S	F	F	U	T	E	S	V	C	N	I	Z	E
A	D	H	P	O	R	A	Q	P	K	I	S	X	S	C	D	M
W	O	T	E	H	K	M	Z	G	N	O	I	T	P	U	R	E
S	S	E	N	K	C	I	S	U	N	G	I	A	P	M	A	C

− 100 −

Here's one final mega crisscross puzzle—and this one is a doozie!

All 45 words and phrases in this puzzle (including the word ALL!) contain a double L. That means there might be a few more overlapping letters than you've dealt with in the other puzzles so far here ... but you're super smart, so you can absolutely solve it!

With so many words to find homes for in the grid, this time the words in the word list have been organized by length to help you find the ones you need more quickly. Good luck!

3 letters
ALL
ELL

4 letters
ALLY
CELL
LULL

5 letters
BRILL
DOLLS
OLLEY
SILLY
SPELL
STALL
TULLE

6 letters
CELLAR
FILLED
ILLEST
MALLOW
NULLED
PAELLA
REALLY
REFILL
TOLLED
WILLOW
YELLOW

7 letters
BELLY-UP
GALLIZE
ICEFALL
ILLOGIC
MISCALL
NETBALL
OUTFALL
SITWELL

8 letters
ALLEY CAT
BACKFILL
GALLEONS
LIBELLEE
OVERALLS
SINFULLY

9 letters
ARMADILLO
DUMBBELLS

13 letters
MISCELLANEOUS

14 letters
ALL GUNS BLAZING
ALL WELL AND GOOD

15 letters
SHILLY-SHALLYING
SMALL-MINDEDNESS

17 letters
PUBLIC OPINION POLL

21 letters
CURIOSITY KILLED THE CAT

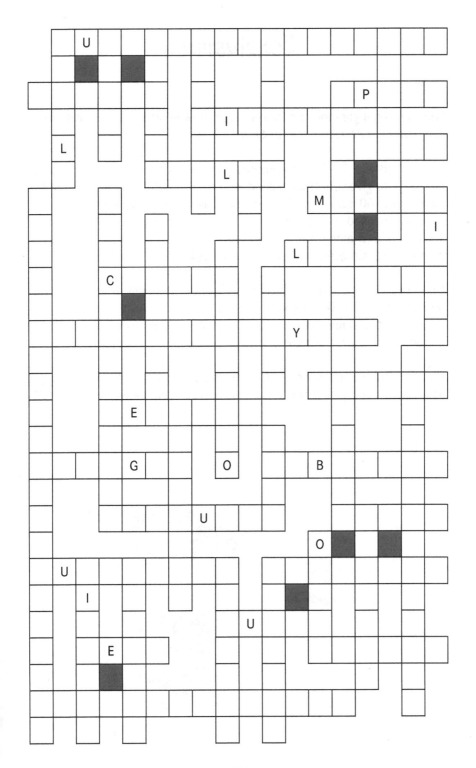

Conclusion

Phew!

With that final gigantic crisscross puzzle now solved, you've completed your *Ultimate Activity Book for Smart Girls!*

So how did you do? Did the puzzles and games here pose enough of a challenge to give your brain a good workout? Hopefully so! And hopefully these past 100 puzzles and games have given you a much needed break and have passed the time too. And who knows—maybe you've learned something new along the way from one of the trivia games, or solved a puzzle or a brain game that you never thought you'd be able to!

Don't worry if you had to resort to peeking at the answers (or jumping onto the internet!) every so often too, of course. After all, there were some very tricky trivia questions and brain teasing challenges here, so getting the odd pointer here and there is to be expected.

Now that we're finished though, it's time to down that pencil, check through your scores, and give that super smart brain of yours a well earned rest!

Solutions

1

```
        F S   B   F L Y   K
  P         R O O   P     C F P
    L     O   O U       F A L
      A T   K   F N     X   S A
      A Z S   W   T W   H S
      V   T A     G A F A V K   T
    E T O M S E H T O L C I   O I
  L   R   S A L O N   W K N N C
E   E         R G G E P H Z   M P
  S E I R E C O R G U M W   N W L
        N E   G T X J Q P F U G A
          L U A D Y   V E   N
        A S T L G Z T F S T
        S A   N A F C U G S
        S   A A C W E O
        F O O D C O U R T S   Z B
        T O L G N I K R A P   E
```

2

8	3	4	2	9	7	6	5	1
2	9	6	5	8	1	3	4	7
7	1	5	6	3	4	8	2	9
6	5	3	8	7	2	9	1	4
9	8	2	1	4	6	5	7	3
4	7	1	9	5	3	2	8	6
5	4	(8)	3	1	9	7	6	2
3	6	7	4	2	5	1	9	8
1	2	9	7	6	8	4	3	5

3

4

P	O	N	B	A	N	G	B
S	A	Y	I	H	C	S	U
Y	M	T	G	N	S	E	N
E	M	A	N	O	B	H	C
T	C	I	L	E	R	P	E
R	I	O	I	X	A	M	R
U	P	N	S	T	I	B	O
O	D	S	N	E	D	S	B

ANSWERS: Ponytail, Bangs, Bunches, Asymmetric, Chignon, Braids, Extensions, Perm, Updo, Bob.

5

FRIEND	CLOTHING ITEM	COLOR
Clara	Bag	Blue
Diedre	T-shirt	Red
Ellie	Shoes	White
Frances	Jacket	Black

6

1	C	A	M	E	R	A
2	H	A	W	A	I	I
3	I	N	C	H	E	S
4	M	E	D	U	S	A
5	P	A	N	A	M	A
6	A	L	B	E	R	T
7	N	E	V	A	D	A
8	Z	E	B	R	A	S
9	E	I	G	H	T	Y
10	E	X	P	I	R	E

ANSWER: Chimpanzee

7

D	O	O	R	W	A	Y		P	A	I	R	S
O		P		R		E		R		G		T
S	P	E	C	I	A	L		O	W	N	E	R
E		R		G		L		U		O		I
S	T	A	N	G		O	R	D	E	R	E	D
				L		W				E		E
P	U	L	L	E	D		G	L	I	D	E	S
U		I		A		A						
D	R	O	O	P	E	D		N	O	S	E	S
D		N		E		V		D		W		A
L	I	E		I	N		I	N	I	T	I	A	L
E		S		N		C		N		N		A
S	A	S	S	Y		E	N	G	A	G	E	D

9

KANSAS and NEVADA

10

Swept under the carpet

11

12

4	2	3	1	9	5	6	7	8
8	1	7	2	3	6	9	5	4
5	9	6	8	7	4	3	1	2
2	6	8	4	5	7	1	3	9
7	3	9	6	2	1	4	8	5
1	5	4	9	8	3	2	6	7
6	4	5	7	1	2	8	9	3
9	7	2	3	6	8	5	4	1
3	8	1	5	4	9	7	2	6

13

14

The **7-letter** word here is Tuesday.

For **6 letters**, there are stayed and steady.

5-letter words include dates, duets, dusty, sated, stead, study and yeast.

For **4 letters**, there are lots of answers including date, days, dues, duet, dust, duty, dyes, east, easy, eats, sate, seat, stay, stud, stye, sued, teas and used.

15

There is only one K and no Os.

16

Gal Gadot = *Wonder Woman*

Kristen Wiig = *Bridesmaids*

Cate Blanchett = *The Lord of the Rings*

Emily Blunt = *A Quiet Place*

Anne Hathaway = *The Devil Wears Prada*

Emma Stone = *La La Land*

Saorsie Ronan = *Lady Bird*

Jennifer Lawrence = *The Hunger Games*

17

B	O	R	E	D		U	S	E	S
R		A		E		T		I	
E	V	I	C	T		J	E	S	T
A		N		E		E			
D			S	M	A	R	T		
	W	R	O	T	E				M
	I		D		S				A
C	O	O	L		D	E	T	E	R
A		T			L		A		C
T	A	S	K		E	A	R	T	H

18

Blue in the face

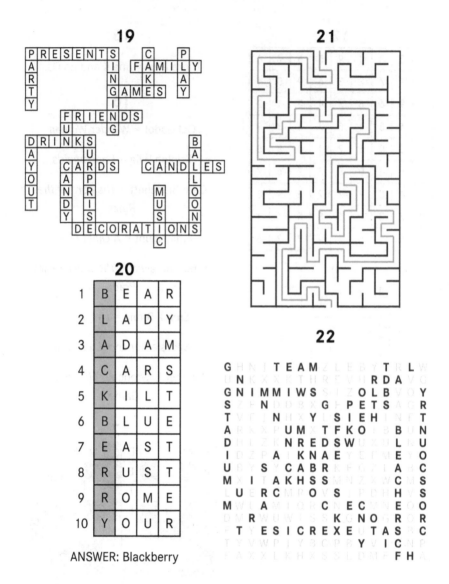

ANSWER: Blackberry

23

9	4	1	6	8	5	7	2	3
8	2	7	3	4	9	6	1	5
6	5	3	1	2	7	8	9	4
5	3	8	7	6	1	9	4	2
1	9	4	2	5	8	3	7	6
2	7	6	4	9	3	5	8	1
7	8	2	5	1	6	4	3	9
3	1	5	9	7	4	2	6	8
4	6	9	8	3	2	1	5	7

26

24

ANSWERS: Vienna, London, Paris, Athens, Copenhagen, Stockholm, Madrid, Lisbon, Brussels, Rome, Amsterdam, Helsinki, Moscow, Minsk, Berlin.

27

28

FIFTEEN and SIXTEEN.

29

There are 19 possible rectangles.

30

e and k

25

SISTER	BOOK	ROOM
Jo	Classic	Bedroom
Kate	Biography	Kitchen
Lena	Adventure	Garden
Michelle	Romance	Lounge

31

ANSWER: Lady Gaga

32

1	4	8	9	7	5	3	6	2
6	2	9	1	4	3	7	5	8
5	3	7	2	6	8	9	1	4
7	5	4	3	9	2	6	8	1
8	1	6	7	5	4	2	3	9
3	9	2	8	1	6	4	7	5
9	7	3	4	8	1	5	2	6
4	6	1	5	2	7	8	9	3
2	8	5	6	3	9	1	4	7

33

34

For **7 letters** here, you can have respect, scepter, or specter.

For **6 letters**, there is creeps, crepes, erects, pester, peters, preset, and secret.

For **5 letters**, there are lots of answers including creep, crepe, crept, crest, erect, peers, peter, reset, spree, steep, steer, terse, and trees.

And for **4 letters**, there are lots of answers too, including cert, peer, pert, pest, pets, reps, rest, sect, seep, seer, step, and tree.

35

W	A	L	L	S	T	R	E	E	T	C	R	A	S	H	
			E												I
	C	L	E	O	P	A	T	R	A		M		W
	I				N						R		O
	V		W		C	O	L	U	M	B	U	S		J
	I		O		I						O		I
V	A	L	K	Y	R	I	E	S		S	A	L	E	M
	W		L		N						E		A
E	A		D		T		M	D	D	A	Y	
T	R		W		E		A			R		J
N		P	A		G		R			Y		O
A		E	R		Y		C					H
M		R			P		O					N
	B	O	S	T	O	N	T	E	A	P	A	R	T	Y	S
	I				O						O
	A	B	R	A	H	A	M	L	I	N	C	O	L	N
					O									

36

Stiletto = Foot

Cloche = Head

Alice band = Hair

Bracelet = Wrist

Culottes = Legs

Ring = Finger

Choker = Neck

Corset = Trunk

37

POLKA, RUMBA, and SALSA.

38

▼

		S	P	I	N	
	W	E	R	E		
M	I	N	I			
			M	A	R	E
S	A	L	E			
			R	O	S	E

ANSWER: Primer

39

There are 18 hair grips.

40

1	B	I	B	L	E
2	A	N	G	L	E
3	R	O	G	E	R
4	B	A	G	E	L
5	I	N	D	I	A
6	E	G	Y	P	T
7	D	I	E	G	O
8	O	P	R	A	H
9	L	A	T	I	N
10	L	O	U	I	S

ANSWER: Barbie doll

41

```
            I N I M E G
S S       S
C   U   C E Z Y C
O   I C A       A S
R   A S R T P   U N
P   I   A   R I Z A C
I P         U R I A O   E
O   A     A Q S C   D   R
A       R T S T A   O L I
  R   T B R U     R   A
    I I   O I R         N   C
      G E L       L U     O E L
    A   O S           A       G
  S   G                   T   R
  Y                           I
        H O R O S C O P E V
```

42

8	6	9	1	4	5	7	3	2
1	3	7	2	8	6	4	5	9
2	4	5	3	7	9	6	8	1
6	5	3	4	2	8	9	1	7
9	1	8	5	6	7	2	4	3
4	7	2	9	3	1	8	6	5
7	9	6	8	5	3	1	2	4
5	2	1	6	9	4	3	7	8
3	8	4	7	1	2	5	9	6

45

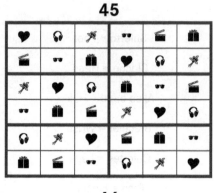

46

Line B

47

Eiffel Tower = Paris

Acropolis = Athens

Liberty Bell = Philadelphia

Space Needle = Seattle

Statue of Liberty = New York

Buckingham Palace = London

Sistine Chapel = Rome

Leaning Tower = Pisa

43

44

M	E	X	I	C	O	R	A
I	A	R	M	A	S	O	N
S	S	S	I	R	E	N	G
S	O	O	R	P	Y	O	E
U	R	C	O	I	N	V	R
R	C	S	D	L	O	E	N
O	D	E	R	E	B	M	E
N	N	O	C	O	W	T	S

48

W	O	O	D	P	K	K	A	B	U
E	C	K	O	E	O	O	R	R	R
A	U	C	O	C	K	E	R	F	L
G	L	E	T	O	U	L	O	M	A
P	E	R	E	G	C	N	O	I	O
P	E	C	A	R	A	E	G	N	G
I	L	L	R	I	N	P	R	E	T
C	A	A	D	N	S	I	G	I	R
N	N	N	I	E	T	K	E	V	E
O	C	L	A	F	O	R	O	N	O

ANSWERS: Woodpecker, Kookaburra, Eagle, Cuckoo, Toucan, Flamingo, Loon, Peregrine falcon, Pelican, Cardinal, Egret, Pigeon, Stork, Vireo.

50

2	7	8	4	3	1	6	5	9
6	5	1	9	7	8	2	4	3
4	3	9	2	5	6	7	1	8
7	8	5	1	6	9	3	2	4
3	4	2	5	8	7	1	9	6
1	9	6	3	4	2	8	7	5
8	6	4	7	2	5	9	3	1
9	2	3	8	1	4	5	6	7
5	1	7	6	9	3	4	8	2

49

```
            M
       E    A B
    R    L U                W
     I  L T       A       H
  N F   I T G     D S W I
 G L   N E N S G G E C O     P
R U O  A R I       O K S W N P
E U  V T T     S C C    G S X I
R    W S  L I O O    N A     N
      O  E F L A    E I L    G
   R  M T O       B K T  C
 F I A E R            A    R
  R R I          B  S E
    N             Y A
C P G                R M
 B A K I N G P O W D E R   U
                           P
```

51

52

53

FRIEND	DOG	BREED
Sandy	Hector	Chihuahua
Candy	Rover	Dachshund
Cindy	Rex	Labrador
Lindy	Timmy	Terrier

54

There are several **7-letters** words here, including rattles, starlet, and startle.

For **6**, there are words like alerts, alters, latest, latter, rattle, salter, staler, taster, and treats.

5-letter words include alert, alter, earls, laser, later, latte, least, rates, slate, stale, stare, start, state, steal, tales, tarts, taste, tears, tesla, and treats.

And there are lots of **4-letter** words here, including ales, arts, earl, ears, east, eats, eras, last, late, lets, rate, rats, real, rest, sale, salt, seal, sear, seat, star, tale, tars, tart, tear, teas, and test.

55

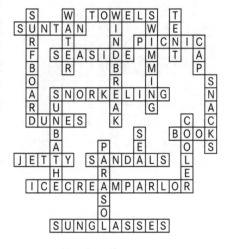

56

There are 17 pencils.

57

T	O	A	S	T		C		D	
I		L		A	N	I	M	A	L
R	E	A	L	M		N		N	
E		R		E	N	E	R	G	Y
D	I	M	E	S		M		L	
	S		Q		B	A	R	E	S
A	S	S	U	M	E		A		A
	U		A		A	T	T	I	C
D	E	A	L	E	R		E		K
	D		S		D	U	S	T	S

58

CANDY, LOLLY, and TAFFY.

59

1. Heart
2. Muscle
3. Shoulder
4. Intestine
5. Stomach

60

1	**C**	A	P	I	T	A	L
2	**I**	T	A	L	I	A	N
3	**N**	U	C	L	E	A	R
4	**D**	I	A	M	O	N	D
5	**E**	Y	E	L	A	S	H
6	**R**	O	L	L	I	N	G
7	**E**	L	E	A	N	O	R
8	**L**	E	B	L	A	N	C
9	**L**	A	D	D	E	R	S
10	**A**	L	A	B	A	M	A

ANSWER: Cinderella

62

8	2	6	4	3	5	1	9	7
1	9	7	8	6	2	4	3	5
5	4	3	7	1	9	6	2	8
7	1	8	2	9	3	5	6	4
6	3	4	5	7	8	2	1	9
9	5	2	1	4	6	7	8	3
3	6	1	9	5	7	8	4	2
4	8	5	3	2	1	9	7	6
2	7	9	6	8	4	3	5	1

61

```
K C O L L U B A R D N A S
  H T R O W S M E H S I R H C
J A K E G Y L L E N H A A L N N H
S                         J I A U
  D                     U   A T G
M   L                 L   A T A H
T   E       O           I   N S L J
N N R   N G A L G A D O T N A I A
U I Y O Y       R       A E H E C
L P       E O         V M H C P K
B S       S B R   E     A A O M
Y I       E T   N S       T C R A
L R       R     R I A       H I T N
I H   T       R E   Y       A S M
M C S         H   E     R   W S A
E             C         P   A E N
      C H R I S P R A T T   Y J
```

ANSWERS: Anne Hathaway, Chris Evans, Chris Hemsworth, Chris Pine, Chris Pratt, Emily Blunt, Gal Gadot, Hugh Jackman, Jake Gyllenhaal, Jessica Chastain, Julia Roberts, Meryl Streep, Natalie Portman, Ryan Reynolds, Sandra Bullock.

63

64

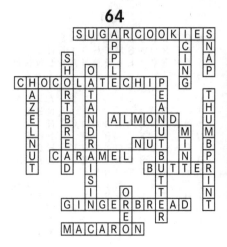

66

W	H	E	N	O	W	H	E
G	R	A	N	D	O	G	R
N	P	O	I	N	T	I	E
U	P	H	T	E	H	G	X
O	A	G	S	N	U	G	A
Y	S	I	R	B	M	L	C
A	I	D	E	D	N	E	T
D	R	E	T	S	E	Y	L

65

Venus Williams = Tennis

Simone Biles = Gymnastics

Megan Rapinoe = Soccer

Nelly Korda = Golf

Lisa Leslie = Basketball

Sha'Carri Richardson = Athletics

Katie Ledecky = Swimming

Claressa Shields = Boxing

67

There is only one letter L, and no letter V

68

C	L	A	S	S
H	■	D	■	P
A	U	D	I	O
F	■	E	■	R
F	I	R	S	T

69

They all begin and end in D: DEMAND, DARTED, DRAPED, DIETED, DASHED, DENIED.

70

FRIEND	MARK	SUBJECT
Amy	D	Geography
Beatrice	A+	Science
Clara	C	Math
Di	A-	History

71

ANSWERS: 1. Examiners, 2. Excavates, 3. Excellent, 4. Excessive, 5. Exchanged, 6. Exclaimed, 7. Excluding, 8. Exercised, 9. Exfoliate, 10. Exhausted, 11. Expelling, 12. Explained, 13. Explosive, 14. Extending, 15. Extracted.

72

73

6	9	7	5	2	1	3	4	8
2	3	8	4	7	9	6	1	5
1	5	4	3	6	8	9	7	2
7	8	5	9	4	2	1	3	6
3	6	9	8	1	7	5	2	4
4	2	1	6	5	3	8	9	7
8	1	2	7	9	6	4	5	3
9	4	3	2	8	5	7	6	1
5	7	6	1	3	4	2	8	9

74

75

C	A	R	C	R	U	E	L	S	U
A	N	D	I	G	B	L	A	N	M
I	T	L	O	A	A	P	S	K	M
H	E	K	O	N	C	L	O	V	E
O	R	W	H	E	E	B	A	E	R
T	A	H	T	W	L	B	D	S	F
Y	M	E	F	O	O	O	D	T	O
O	E	D	O	O	V	O	L	O	R
U	D	O	T	D	E	R	Y	R	T
M	A	O	U	S	T	H	G	I	N

ANSWERS: Cardigan, Cruel Summer, Anti-Hero, Blank Space, Love Story, Look What You Made Me Do, Out of the Woods, Bad Blood, Fortnight, Lover.

76
LASAGNA and FUSILLI

77
Sail the seven seas

78

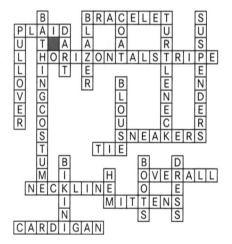

79

The **7-letter** word here is rejects.

The **6-letter** words could be ejects, erects, jester, reject or secret.

Some of the **5-letter** words you can make include crest, eject, erect, jeers, reset, scree, steer and trees.

The **4-letter** words include cert, jeer, jest, jets, recs, rest, sect, seer, tees and trees.

80

1	S	A	L	E	M
2	H	E	A	R	T
3	A	R	E	N	A
4	K	O	A	L	A
5	E	I	G	H	T
6	I	N	D	I	A
7	T	E	X	A	S
8	O	S	C	A	R
9	F	I	F	T	H
10	F	R	O	D	O

ANSWER: Shake It Off

81

ANSWERS: ATHENS Greece, DUBLIN Ireland, HAVANA Cuba, ISTANBUL Turkey, LONDON United Kingdom, NAIROBI Kenya, PARIS France, RIO DE JANEIRO Brazil, SHANGHAI China, STOCKHOLM Sweden, SYDNEY Australia, VANCOUVER Canada.

82

5	3	8	7	6	4	1	9	2
4	2	1	5	9	8	7	3	6
6	7	9	1	2	3	8	4	5
2	9	5	4	1	7	6	8	3
8	4	3	6	5	2	9	7	1
7	1	6	3	8	9	5	2	4
9	6	2	8	4	5	3	1	7
1	8	7	2	3	6	4	5	9
3	5	4	9	7	1	2	6	8

83

84

Katy Perry = Smile

Adele = 30

The Weeknd = After Hours

Taylor Swift = Midnights

Beyoncé = Cowboy Carter

Ariana Grande = Eternal Sunshine

Olivia Rodrigo = Guts

SZA = SOS

85

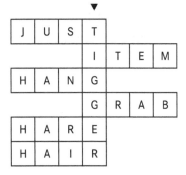

ANSWER: Tigger

86

90

ANSWER: Musical instrument

87

C	O	L	O	R	I	G	H
E	A	R	L	Y	E	A	T
R	P	E	A	R	L	R	H
A	O	T	O	D	O	O	E
T	R	H	Y	A	C	T	R
S	D	G	I	L	A	H	E
R	E	L	I	M	S	I	A
E	B	B	O	R	E	T	S

88

f and l

89

There are 20 leaves.

91

P	R	O	B	L	E	M		P	O	S	E	R
A		S		U		A		L		A		E
C	H	A	N	G	E	S		E	A	S	E	D
E		K		G		S		A		H		F
D	R	A	M	A		A	N	T	H	I	L	L
				G		C				M		A
S	P	I	N	E	C	H	I	L	L	I	N	G
T		N				U		O				
R	E	S	U	L	T	S		N	O	T	E	S
I		T		E				G		E		P
P	L	A	Z	A		T	E	E	N	A	G	E
E		L		S		S		S		C		L
S	P	L	I	T		S	A	T	C	H	E	L

92

2	1	5	8	7	9	6	3	4
6	9	3	5	4	1	8	2	7
4	8	7	3	6	2	1	9	5
5	7	8	2	1	6	9	4	3
3	6	4	9	5	7	2	8	1
1	2	9	4	3	8	5	7	6
7	4	2	6	8	5	3	1	9
8	5	1	7	9	3	4	6	2
9	3	6	1	2	4	7	5	8

93

94

B	E	Y	P	I	N	L	A	D	Y
T	A	O	H	A	K	S	T	Y	G
L	Y	N	D	R	R	Y	E	L	A
O	É	C	U	A	L	I	S	A	G
R	O	L	I	V	I	P	A	C	H
S	R	D	O	R	A	E	P	P	A
W	I	K	E	S	H	L	L	R	O
I	G	O	B	I	A	A	D	E	A
F	T	L	I	L	L	L	E	L	N
H	S	I	E	E	I	I	Z	Z	O

ANSWERS: Beyoncé, Pink, Lady Gaga, Taylor Swift, Harry Styles, Dua Lipa, Olivia Rodrigo, Chappell Roan, Kesha, Billie Eilish, Adele, Lizzo.

95

The **7-letter word** here is airport.

For **6**, there are parrot and raptor.

5-letter words include patio, prior, ratio, and tapir.

And for **4**, there are lots of words including atop, pair, part, port, riot, roar, tarp, trap, trio, and trip.

96

Lithe = Flexible
Listless = Weary
Lexicon = Vocabulary
Labyrinth = Maze
Laborious = Difficult
Languish = Weaken
Luminary = Star
Lampoon = Sendup

97

1	S	A	H	A	R	A
2	T	A	U	R	U	S
3	U	N	I	T	E	D
4	P	I	E	R	R	E
5	I	M	E	L	D	A
6	D	A	N	I	E	L
7	I	T	H	A	C	A
8	S	A	T	U	R	N
9	A	V	E	N	U	E
10	S	E	R	E	N	A
11	S	H	A	N	I	A
12	T	W	E	L	V	E
13	U	R	S	U	L	A
14	P	O	L	A	N	D
15	I	M	P	O	R	T
16	D	I	S	N	E	Y
17	D	A	M	S	E	L
18	O	R	E	G	O	N
19	E	D	I	S	O	N
20	S	H	E	R	Y	L

ANSWER: Stupid is as stupid does

98

PERSON	DRINK	EXTRA	SNACK
Mom	Macchiato	To go	Brownie
Dad	Cappuccino	Decaf	Muffin
Son	Mocha	Extra shot	Cookie
Daughter	Latte	Hazelnut syrup	Donut

99

```
P           P E R S O N A L     S
B I R T H D A Y D E G   G G N L U
  N         E D V N N N N E I R
  R Y P   T U   I I O I I K A V
H   E   O A T M A T D I P K A T I
I     A L I I T   I L T P N T K V
G     O T L N   S I C O I S C A
G   S L I U P T   O U E H R I O L
L I A T O P R A T P B L S D M C C
E   A M   O H E R C   E   V F O
D R     R   Y C A E     O O M
Y       T   D O L R   L R P
E G A I R R A M   R V L I   C E U
    E G N A H C X E O E E D A N T
    L A C I M E H C   G R L N S E
      E T E L P M O C E Y I I R
    N A T I O N A L     N C C
```

```
              T G N I B M I L C
S T N E D U T S N T C N I C E R P
  R E G N A R T S E     O   P P
    C O M F O R T S M M   Y A R
    M A T E R I A L P U D I O S Y
    P O S I T I O N O   E N P   T
              N   T U C L T E O I N P
Y K   L W I   N C G I R   T M E E
C E G A L A D O G N T D N   R S N
A Y N S A T I I G Y I E E O   E I
R B I O T N P T     D T X N S R C
U O K P I U   S R I   I S R T P I
C A N O P O   E   E D   E N A   D
C R I R S F   U   E S V   I   E
A D H P O     Q   I S         M
    T   H         N O I T P U R E
S S E N K C I S U N G I A P M A C
```

100

100

Made in United States
Troutdale, OR
12/19/2024